invite
PRESS

HEIRS

◇ — OF — ◇

EDEN

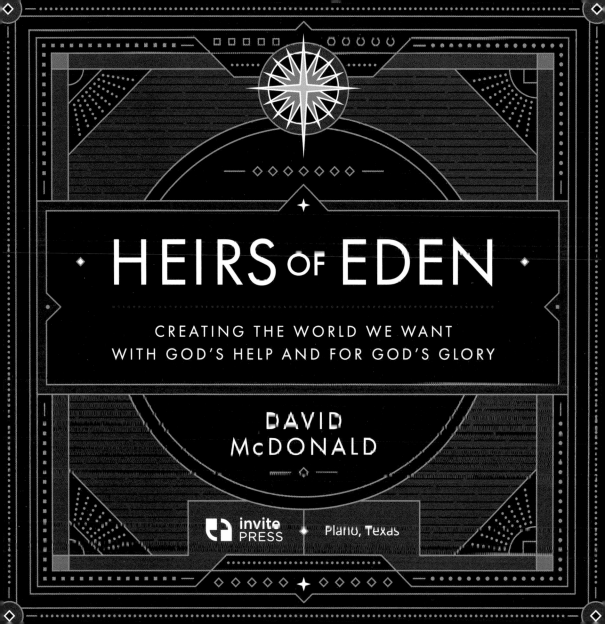

HEIRS OF EDEN

CREATING THE WORLD WE WANT WITH GOD'S HELP AND FOR GOD'S GLORY

DAVID McDONALD

invite
PRESS ◆ Plano, Texas

Heirs Of Eden | Creating The World We Want With God's Help And For God's Glory

Copyright 2022 by David McDonald.
Book design and Illustrations by Diana McKnight.
The author retains sole copyright to the materials.

All rights reserved.
No part of this work may be reproduced or transmitted in any form or by any means, electronic or mechanical, including photocopying and recording, or by any information storage or retrieval system, except as may be expressly permitted by the 1976 Copyright Act or in writing from the publisher. Requests for permission can be addressed to Permissions, Invite Press, PO Box 260917, Plano, TX 75026.

This book is printed on acid-free, elemental chlorine-free paper.

ISBN | 978-1-953495-28-0

Scripture quotations, unless otherwise noted, are taken from the Holy Bible, New Living Translation, copyright © 1996, 2004, 2015 by Tyndale House Foundation. Used by permission of Tyndale House Publishers, Carol Stream, Illinois 60188. All rights reserved.

Scripture quotations marked NIV are taken from the Holy Bible, New International Version®, NIV®. Copyright © 1973, 1978, 1984, 2011 by Biblica, Inc.™ Used by permission of Zondervan. All rights reserved worldwide. www.zondervan.com. The "NIV" and "New International Version" are trademarks registered in the United States Patent and Trademark Office by Biblica, Inc.™

Scripture quotations marked KJV are from the King James or Authorized Version of the Bible.

21 22 23 24 25 26 27 28 29 30—10 9 8 7 6 5 4 3 2 1
MANUFACTURED in the UNITED STATES of AMERICA

Visit Dr. David McDonald's website at www.doctordavidmcdonald.com.

For more information on Dr. McDonald's headquarters for innovation visit www.fossoreschapterhouse.com.

WHERE WE WILL GO

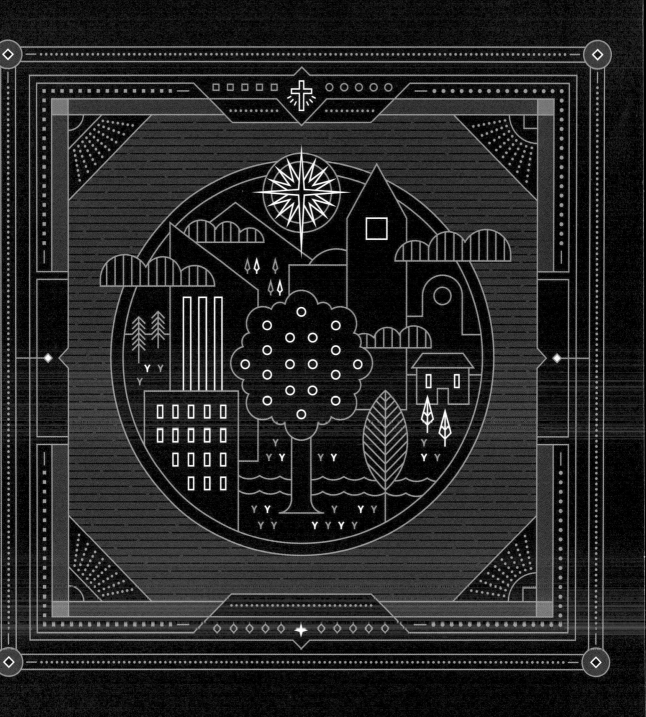

A PUNCH
IN THE
MOUTH

§ My brothers and sisters, lend me your minds. Get sharp! Hearken, and attend!

The world, and the work, is ours.

That declaration ought to bow you in the paunch. Learn it. Know it. Absorb it into every follicle, every eyelash, every tattoo, and every nail. God made the world but didn't finish it. It's a relay race, not a Christmas present. It's an opportunity, not an accommodation. It's your mission, your mandate, your joy, and your hope to work with God and enhance the earth. Make the world truer. Make it more beautiful. Make it more spectacular, more wonderful, more genuine, more adventurous, and more inspiring.

But you've got to do the work.

That's hard to accept. I know you'll have a million questions that I can't answer in a few short sentences. That's why I'm giving you this book. These pages reveal a lifetime of discovery—biblical and theological, personal and creative, relational and civil—all rolled into one spiritual thought grenade: it's up to you.

With God's help. For God's glory.

The world and the work is ours.

And what do I mean when I say "work"?

Work is what we do. It's the term the Bible uses for how we live, for our contribution, for our investment in the people around us and ourselves.

You might, at first, think that's strange. Most people hate to work. They think of work as something to be avoided. Until you dig a little deeper. Then you discover there's work they love. Work they cannot wait to perform. That's the good stuff. That's the true work.

After all, what are people for?

Why are we here? Why were we made? What makes us the same, and what differentiates us from one another?

God made the world, loves the world, entered the world, and works to redeem the world. God always does this through people. Yes, always. God is so committed to people that God became a person, not only to demonstrate how people should thrive but also to provide a means for all people to fulfill our divine destiny, to experience our original intention, to satisfy our ultimate ardor, to offer us the hope of a better world, a world we create along with God.

If these ideas sound foreign, allow me to put your mind at ease. These thoughts aren't about earning entrance into heaven, or convincing God you're special, or justifying your eternality with achievement. These ideas concern working alongside God to enjoy life as you envision it in your dreams, as you imagine life ripening with justice and beauty, fascination and peace. And you will never enjoy that life if you fail to work for it. Life comes to us as breath, but if

we never exercise our lungs we won't learn to swim in the depths nor scale the mountain heights. Life is meant for living, and abundant life comes to those who grasp the hand of their Creator and join in the ongoing work of Creation.

In these pages, you'll explore scripture through a lens of human development, promise, and hope. It would be a mistake to assume *human* somehow means "absent God's involvement."

Quite the contrary. We cannot be human without God. Not wholly. Not quite.

This book is meant as a guide to help you figure out what you can do and who God is calling you to become. Stop waiting for someone else to fix you, save you, heal you, diagnose you, nurture you, or pacify you. You are a torrent of holy fire, a storm of sanctified provocation. Let the scripture teach you why. Let me tell you how.

And, when you encounter those theological hiccups and philosophical impossibilities that will inevitably disrupt you, press on. Push through. Question. Argue. Shout. Rage. Because your fury, and your fervor, serve God. So, get angry. Get worked up. And channel that energy into making a better world.

After all . . . that's why you're here.

D.

The Bible begins in a Garden

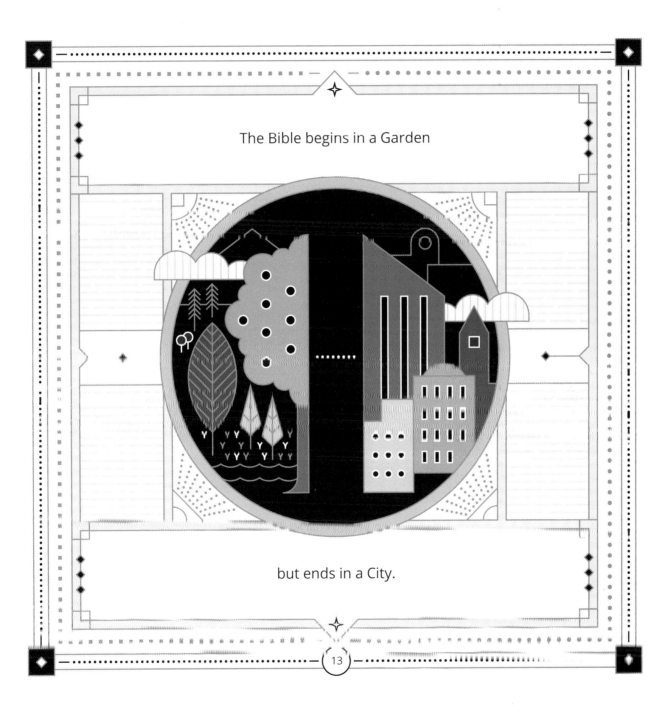

but ends in a City.

Why?

Why doesn't the Bible conclude back in the Garden?

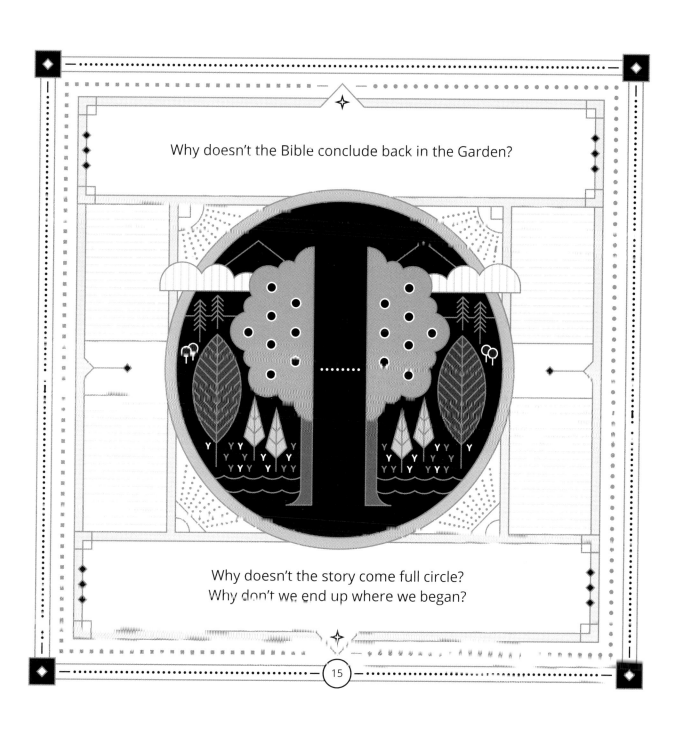

Why doesn't the story come full circle?
Why don't we end up where we began?

Shouldn't the biblical story be cyclical?
Isn't that what we're taught,
that we can get back what we've lost?

That nothing is gone forever?
That we can be redeemed?

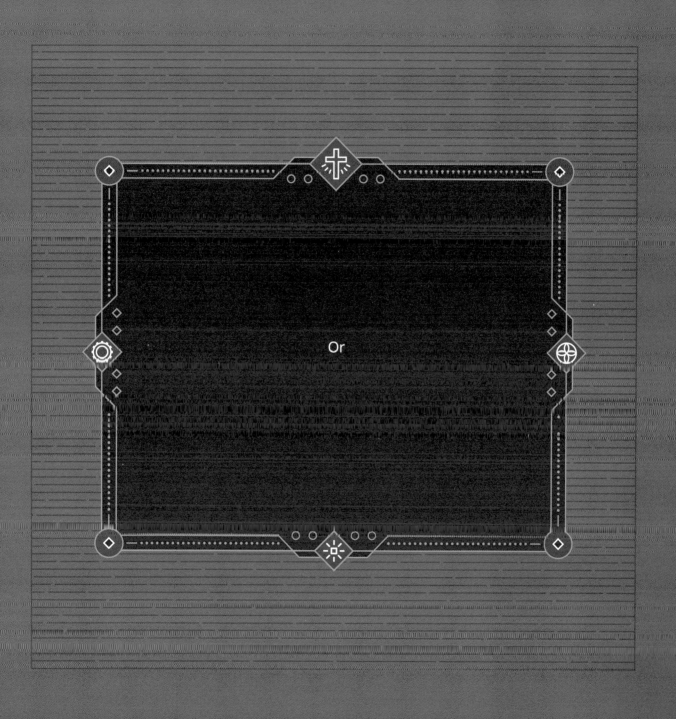

Or

Maybe God wants us to know we can never go back.
Not to the past. Not to the way things were

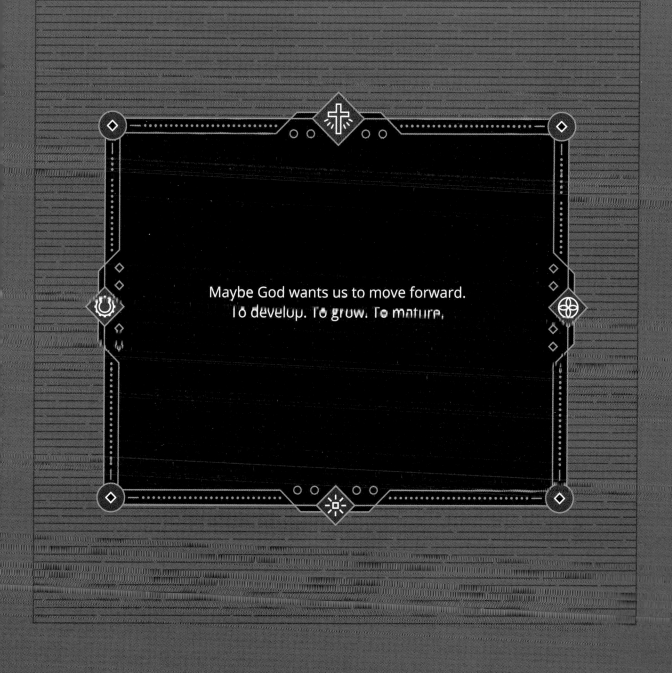

Maybe God wants us to move forward.
To develop. To grow. To mature.

Maybe God inhabits the future,
summoning us onward.

Maybe God's Garden ripens into God's City.

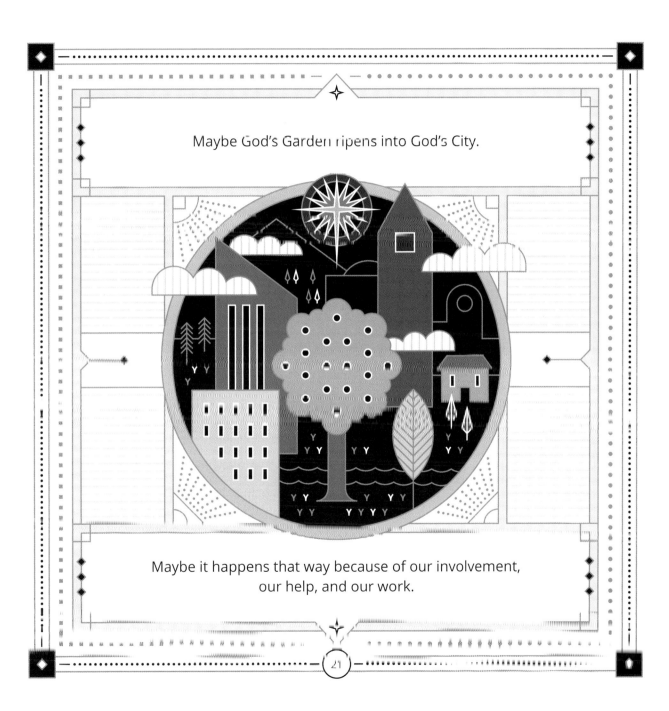

Maybe it happens that way because of our involvement,
our help, and our work.

Maybe we're meant to develop our homes?
To grow them? To cultivate our property and culture,
our rituals and relationships, such that our homes
function as a microcosm of God's plans for the Earth?

Maybe we're meant to deepen our investments
with our neighbors and peers, our coworkers and colleagues?

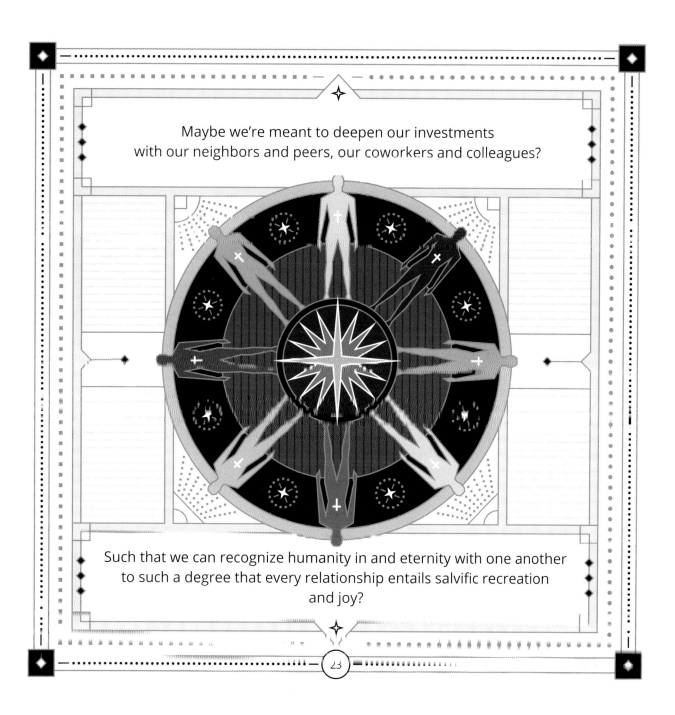

Such that we can recognize humanity in and eternity with one another
to such a degree that every relationship entails salvific recreation
and joy?

We were made by God to be like God.[1] We're God's emissaries,[2] people made in the divine image, God's shadows.[3] As Athanasius of Alexandra famously stated, "God was made man that we might be made God."[4] As God's co-creators, we are meant to expand the borders of Eden, to fill the Earth and to subdue it[5] until the glory of God covers the Earth.[6] That includes cultivating God's government,[7] God's creativity,[8] and God's peace, which will require us to not only draw together the resources of Creation[9] but to generate wise order and release human potential.[10]

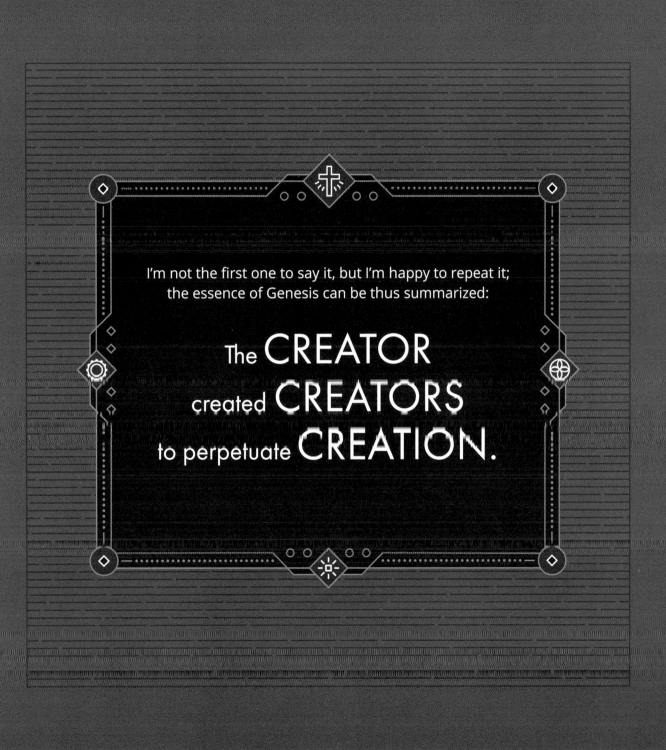

I'm not the first one to say it, but I'm happy to repeat it; the essence of Genesis can be thus summarized:

The CREATOR created CREATORS to perpetuate CREATION.

We were made to do things. Not just to be. Not simply to exist, but to live, to dream, to draw together the resources of Creation, to generate wise order, and to release human potential.

To rule. To reign.

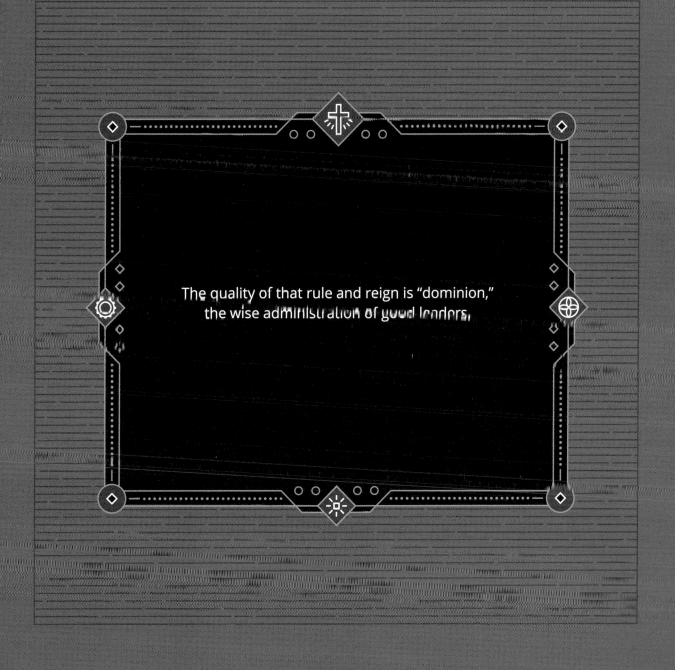

The quality of that rule and reign is "dominion," the wise administration of good leaders.

How is wise rule evaluated?
How do we manifest benevolence?
Godliness? Justice?

A weak ruler refuses to grow roses because of the thorns.
A good ruler plants rose gardens.
A great ruler makes rosaries.

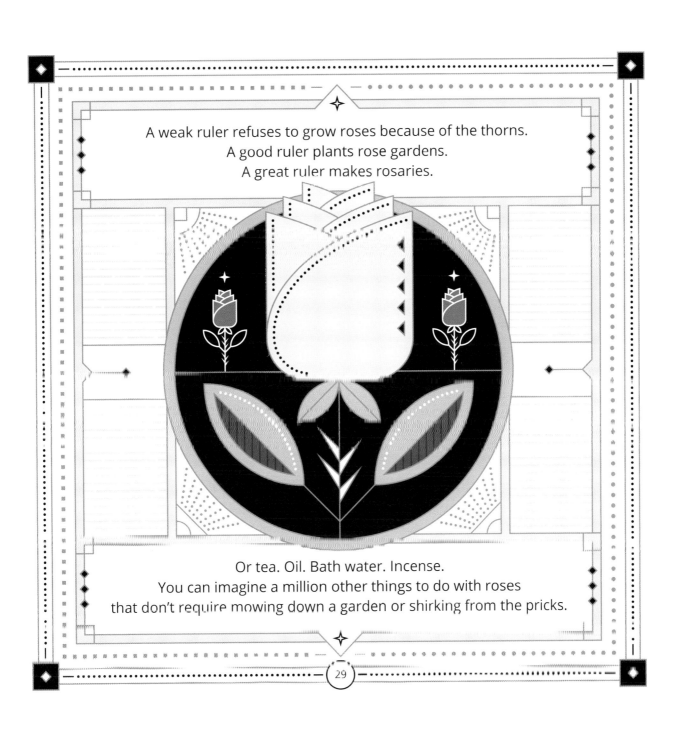

Or tea. Oil. Bath water. Incense.
You can imagine a million other things to do with roses
that don't require mowing down a garden or shirking from the pricks.

One metaphor the Bible uses to describe our work with God in expanding Creation—the specifically human portion of that work—is "the City."[11]

Cities are the product of our cooperation with God.
They refer to places of imagination, agency, and relationship
where humanity gathers and societies flourish.

That's why the final picture in the Bible is of the New Jerusalem,
a Garden-City that covers the Earth.[12]

God gave us a Garden[13]
but requires from us a City.[14]

We are the City of God.[15] We are a living temple.[16] God lives in us.[17] God is home with us.[18] God is both master builder[19] and chief cornerstone.[20][21]

That the Bible begins in a Garden and concludes in a City
demonstrates that God's purposes are not cyclical,
but developmental.

God doesn't make us endlessly repeat life's lessons,
but leads us through a long process of maturation,
resulting in our final and eventual perfection.

This is our destiny: to become
the best possible version of ourselves.

With God's help. For God's glory.

We grow as we work alongside our Creator.
We stretch to reach God, knowing we
won't get all the way there, but also knowing
that unless we stretch, we languish.

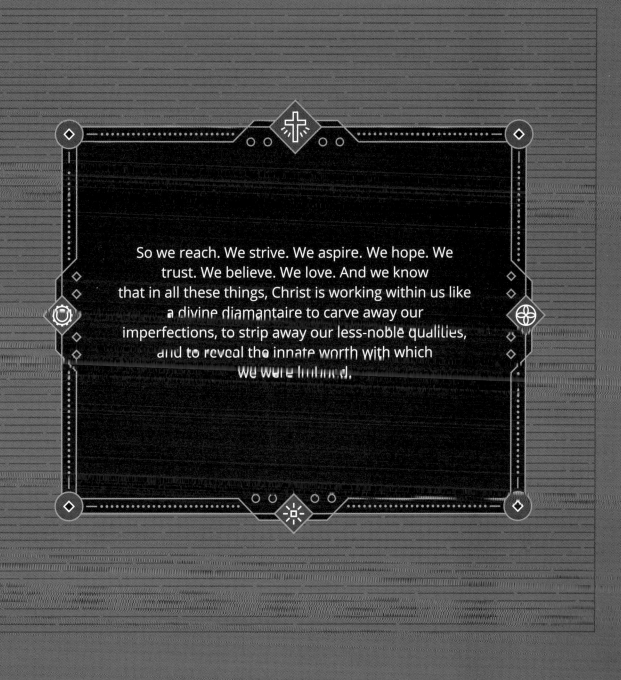

So we reach. We strive. We aspire. We hope. We
trust. We believe. We love. And we know
that in all these things, Christ is working within us like
a divine diamantaire to carve away our
imperfections, to strip away our less-noble qualities,
and to reveal the innate worth with which
we were imbued.

God is not making you all over again;
God is making you anew.

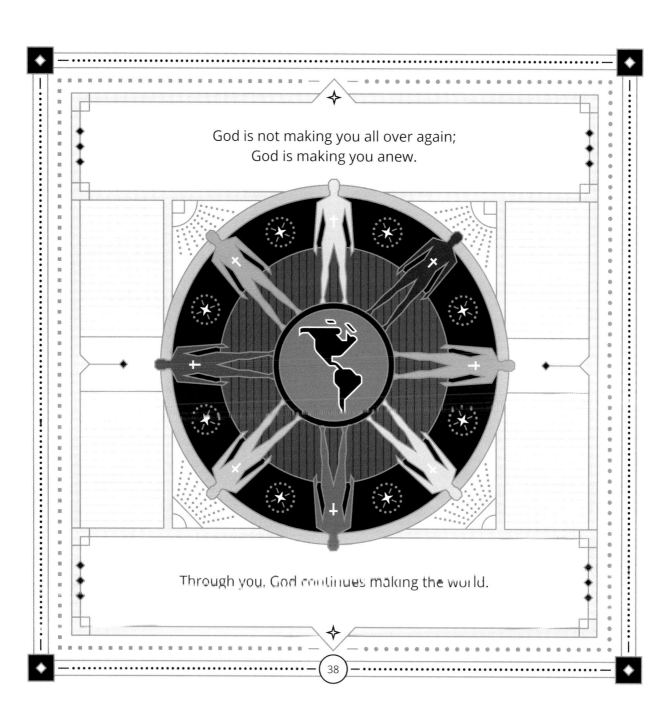

Through you, God continues making the world.

The Spirit of God is forming us into people who can love the unlovely, enjoy wealth even when poor, rejoice in the midst of suffering, and defy death because the life of Christ lives in us forevermore.

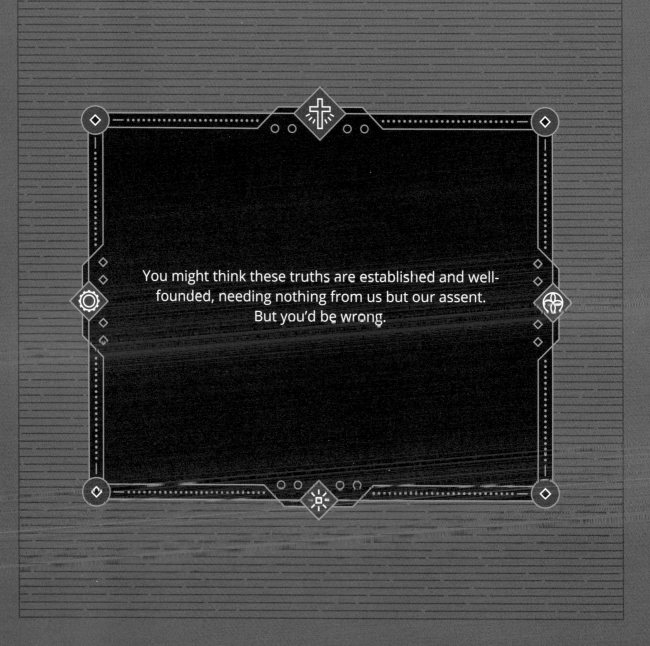

You might think these truths are established and well-founded, needing nothing from us but our assent. But you'd be wrong.

We are asleep. We are tired. We are convinced that what we do matters little, if at all. We watch as governments and celebrities dictate what we are permitted to enjoy, and we must be roused.

We must be revived.

This book is your manifesto for living, for acting,
for choosing, for creating, for dreaming,
and for cooperating with God to heal the world.

It's *our* world. God made the world *for us.*
God conceived a world we get to keep creating.

WE are the HEIRS of EDEN.

So let's get to work.

The world isn't yet the one we want. It's rife with consumerism and greed, racial prejudice and political injustice. It's a world of corruption and malfeasance, depravity and gore. And our disgust with the state of this world is not a dissatisfaction with her Creator, but with our failure to continue manifesting beauty, truth, and goodness as God intended. Both our passivity and our deviance have allowed the world to deteriorate from a planetary paradise into something resembling a cosmic apple core.

But good news: we get to fix it.

Because the world, and the work, is ours.

FLOURISH

✦ We believe in a Creator, a Maker, a Sustainer, and Revealer of Worlds who rules the cosmos and is Lord over Creation. **This Creator perfectly designed our world so we might flourish within it.**

Read that again. *You were made to flourish.*

You weren't made to be bored. To comply. To flounder. To diminish. You weren't created to be one of those who sardonically and unoriginally lament they are "living the dream" while working sad hours at an inconvenience store.

You were made to experience the best quality of life imaginable. Life, and life more abundant. Electric life. Excitable life. Life accelerated and enthused.

In the beginning, our Creator placed a Garden in the center of Creation, calling the Garden *Eden*. Eden was a paradise. God placed our ancestral parents within that place, and Eden was where *we* walked with God.

We walked with God—we were not made to sit, but to walk, not with deadbeats or dullards, but with the divine.

Don't you see? You have been created with a destiny and a calling and a yearning and a purpose for the extraordinary. You were placed within paradise, and paradise calls you home. Paradise calls you up from the sofa, out of the house, away from the norm and the safe and the bland, so you can keep step with the Spirit and survey the sacred landscape of the earth.

Your life is not yet what it may become.

Never forget who you are and where you come from. It changes things. It did for me. I used to think I was from Vancouver, but passports from Eden have better stamps. They bear the thumbprint of God.

And so do you.

For the Lord is God, and he created the heavens
and Earth and put everything in place.

He made the world to be lived in, not to be a place
of empty chaos.

"I am the Lord," he says, "and there is no other.

"I publicly proclaim bold promises. I do not whisper
obscurities in some dark corner.

"I would not have told the people of my land to seek me
if I could not be found.

"I, the Lord, speak only what is true and declare only
what is right."

Isaiah 45:18–19

CREATE. DREAM. ENJOY!

† How long do you think Adam and Eve lived in Eden before they were expelled? And, during that time, what kind of work do you think they enjoyed alongside God?

If, as scripture maintains, they were tasked with "subduing the earth," don't you think that means they were working on it? And what would that work entail? At the very least, landscaping—clearing trees, moving plants and shrubs, creating trailways and walkways, getting access to water and light. And what would their landscaping look like, these people living in the ancient Near East?

It's possible that we already know.

Ancient Near Eastern gardens were not undeveloped wilderness but "expansive urban parks."[22] That means they had architecture and engineering, pathways and pergolas, gazebos and vistas galore. Eden wasn't a jungle. It would have been closer to the Hanging Gardens or English botanical gardens. It was a place Adam and Eve continued to cultivate after God first created the world.

God gave the flowers, then we made the bouquet.

The word *paradise* is Persian for "garden."[23] In the ancient world, gardens were essential components of religious worship. Most Eastern temples had gardens, and priests considered these gardens to be the place where the gods rested.

Why do gods need rest?

According to legend, gods spend most of their existence beating each other into submission. That's why so many creation myths involve one god dominating another. In Egypt, the priests told the people that Amun forced all other gods to submit; in Babylon, it was Marduk who conquered Tiamat.[24]

But God—our God, the True God of gods and Lord of All—did not need to recover from conflict. Our God has no equal. Does a lion skirmish with a gnat? Does a snake train for war with a snail? No. Our God made the world with divine Word. The Maker sang Creation into existence, a melody of blessing amid the harmony of living things, born upon the rhythm of the stars.

"Eden was the archetypal temple,"[25] a Garden paradise where God walked with humanity in the cool of the day. Genesis 3 depicts God's relationship with humanity as personal, filial, and exploratory. In that chapter, both God and God's people moved freely through the Garden, pursuing their interests and their pleasures in concert with their work. The "rest" God shared was not inactivity. On the contrary, all activity was a manifestation of vocation, obedience, and delight. Leviticus 26 returns to this imagery, envisioning a time when people would return to this Garden lifestyle, hoping and trusting that God will provide something Edenic once again.

The Creator created Eden as a garden of divine rest. Again, rest does not mean inactivity. Rest is the catchall term for leisure and pleasure in abundance, doing work that we choose among people who care. God didn't need a break from battle, but chose to set an example for enjoyment, fecundity, and mutuality. Rest is holy. Rest is godly. **Our lives are tiresome, and if we become rest-less we also become anxious, agitated, and dis-eased.**

The important thing to remember is that the value of rest does not negate the virtue of work. There is a sacerdotal rhythm to our lives that authenticates sublime work and righteous rest. The two exist in tandem, with neither securing pride of place. And since this book will largely focus on holy work, let us early establish that rest must also be esteemed.

Eden was a place of rest for God and for people, a place where we could be with our Maker forever.

Yes—forever. All six of the prior days in Creation's story have a conclusion. But the seventh day never ends. We are meant to live in eternal rest with God.

And what were we meant to do forever from this reservoir of rest?

Create. Dream. Make. Design. Build. And enjoy!

God created a paradise for us to share, enjoying rest our Creator didn't need, after forgoing a contest our Lord couldn't have lost.

From this superabundance of boundless energy and passion, we can do anything we wish

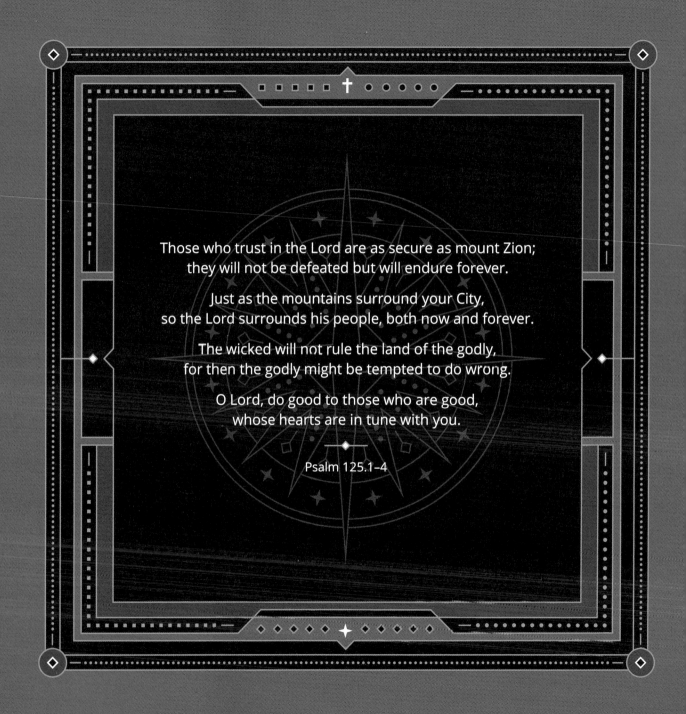

Those who trust in the Lord are as secure as mount Zion;
they will not be defeated but will endure forever.

Just as the mountains surround your City,
so the Lord surrounds his people, both now and forever.

The wicked will not rule the land of the godly,
for then the godly might be tempted to do wrong.

O Lord, do good to those who are good,
whose hearts are in tune with you.

Psalm 125.1–4

ORIGINAL BLESSING

⟡ Eden was a temple, and ancient temples needed two things: priests and idols. The idols contained the deity's presence and the priests mediated that presence for the people.

That right there is our first clue about who we are and what we're meant to enjoy. Creation isn't merely about dignity— being made in God's image —but equally about purpose and imagination. We were designed with dreams, hints of possibility and holiness, exploration and wonder.

Genesis tells us **God made humanity in the divine image and likeness.** That word "image" is the Hebrew word *tselem*, but it's best translated "idol."[26] That's right. We are God's idols. **Whenever people see us, they're supposed to realize they're in the presence of God.** This is the reason for the many prohibitions in scripture against idolatry. Other idols— little wooden statues or stone golems —can't think, can't speak, and can't act. But God—our God—wants idols that move. **The only way God wants to be represented in the world is through you.**

One of the many functions of the priesthood in the ancient Near East—regardless of ethnic or religious affiliation—was to guard the temple, to watch it, and to keep it. Many priests were warriors and wardens, guardians and protectors, charged with securing the temple treasury against thieves and the temple sanctuary against blasphemers.

God combined the role of priest and idol. Adam was a priest of the divine presence[27] who served and guarded God's temple.

In Eden, we find all our loves conflated—the ideals of virtue and genius entwined with power and protection. We are knights and gardeners, creatives and chevaliers.

Biblical scholar G. K. Beale claims this guardianship[28] was also intellectual. Guarding the minds of Eden's inhabitants logically included "Adam's teaching of God's Law" to the other members of Creation so they might continue to cultivate the presence of God.[29]

Like Adam, we are God's priest-protectors.[30] We are the locus of God's presence on earth. We are meant to direct others to worship God and to remind them of the divine presence wherever we go.

Once upon a time, we thought the purpose of Genesis was to teach us that humanity sinned and had been separated from God. But how you begin often determines how you conclude, and it's a relief to know sin is not our starting point but a detour Christ corrects. We assumed we lived in a slum of debauchery and vice. Isn't it better to learn the truth? That we were born into paradise as guardians of the Garden? Protectors and progenitors of paradise? That Genesis isn't the story of Original Sin, but of Original Blessing?[31]

Then God said, "Let us make human beings in our
image, to be like us. They will reign over the fish
in the sea, the birds in the sky, the livestock, all the
wild animals on the earth, and the small animals
that scurry along the ground."

So God created human beings in his own image.
In the image of God he created them;
male and female he created them.

Then God blessed them and said, "Be fruitful and
multiply. Fill the earth and govern it. Reign over
the fish in the sea, the birds in the sky, and all the
animals that scurry along the ground."

Genesis 1:26–28

WE GET TO MAKE IT UP

✧ God gave Adam and Eve a mandate to fill the earth and govern it,[32] to have dominion over all living things. Our Creator also tasked Adam with naming the animals and showed neither interest nor impulse in influencing Adam's choices nor learning of them beforehand.[33]

God allowed Adam to cooperate in the work of Creation

Do you see what this means? Creation wasn't finished on the seventh day. God intentionally left some parts undone—naming and subduing at the very least, though we'll see there are many more—so we might have the pleasure of creating alongside our Creator. **When God made us to be like God, that included space for us to create.**

The work of naming was Adam's, just as the work today of programming and patenting, studying and designing, imaging and fostering is ours.

Remember, Eden was one space within Creation, just one specific area. I like to envision it as a hillock—an elevated plot overlooking the rest of Creation, which helps me visualize the

relative smallness of the Garden. When God told Adam and Eve to fill the earth and subdue it, we've got to picture them looking out from that hillock over the untamed wilderness bordering Eden. The holy couple might have looked toward God, incredulously, asking, "All that? You sure?" and God would have replied, "Did I stutter?"

Our spiritual ancestors were tasked with a quest of some enormity, requiring the aid of their ingenuity, their intellect, and their descendants to see it completed. Their mandate wasn't simply to march into the wild and tame a few birds. Nor was it merely a request from God to map out a pathway to the sea, leaving all wilderness untouched. This task would be accomplished by far more "than farming or husbandry; [it would include] the founding of the first city [as one of the] first achievements of [humanity's] enduring mandate to expand the borders of the garden."[34]

Here, then, is our first glimpse at what will become the City of God. **The Garden God gave, coupled with the achievements of humanity, will result in the Garden-City of divine-human cooperation.**

This will be an adventure. There will be danger;[35] this will be difficult; to succeed we will need every ounce of skill, resourcefulness, and courage with which God has gifted us, and that still won't be enough!

God has set us upon a path that only God can navigate.[36] The good news is God isn't looking for passengers but for partners in the work of Creation. **We have been called to draw together the resources of Creation, to bring wise order to the Garden, and to release human potential.**

We are creators created by the Creator to perpetuate Creation

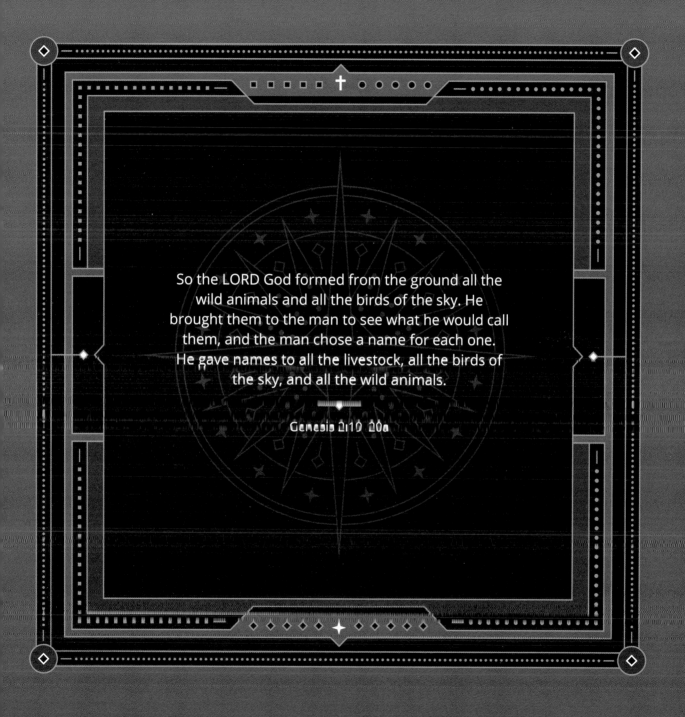

So the LORD God formed from the ground all the wild animals and all the birds of the sky. He brought them to the man to see what he would call them, and the man chose a name for each one. He gave names to all the livestock, all the birds of the sky, and all the wild animals.

Genesis 2:19-20a

LIFE OFFERS NO FULFILLMENT
WITHOUT WORK

People sometimes imagine Heaven as blissful boredom in much the same way they imagine Eden as a petting zoo. But we know differently.

In fact, everyone knows differently. No one has ever sat on a sofa for hours and hours and felt invigorated. No one sleeps till midafternoon and wakes feeling energetically inspired to attack their goals. Sitting is the new smoking. The couch is cancer. Listlessness is the companion of inactivity, and malaise the reward of the sloth. It is only when we choose work that we love that we understand our actions have meaning and our efforts bear fruit that delights, satiates, stimulates, and rewards.

From the beginning, God put it in us that we should contribute. **Creation is an unfinished symphony,** and God has passed us both the fountain pen and the conductor's baton to scribble in the final lines.

Work satisfies, because **work provides dignity.** Work allows us to make a contribution, to feel significant, and to find meaning in the expanse of our minds. Should it come as any surprise that God made us this way?

Robert Lupton, president of Focus Community Strategies and author of *Toxic Charity*, says "Life offers no fulfillment without work,"[37] and that "the creation of productive, meaningful employment fulfills one of the Creator's highest designs."[38]

Why is this so difficult for us to remember? The Hebrew word *avodah* can be translated as both "work" and "worship."[39] Why do so many people insist on vilifying work and sanctifying singing, when the biblical vocabulary clearly indicates that any activity can be sacralized as an offering unto God?

And work, remember, can be anything! Work is something difficult. Good work—great work— is difficulty we select for ourselves. Painting can be a pain or a passion, just as business can be a burden or a blessing. Wisdom demands we reframe our duties as delights, just as maturity allows us to perceive that we are always free to pursue that which we love!

If we do not work, something begins to deteriorate within us. When people who routinely ask for handouts come back again and again and again for more free things, they grow increasingly resentful that they cannot appreciate what they want. Often these same people have the opportunity to work but perceive the work that's available as beneath them and would rather do nothing than earn something, since nothing will allow them to have more. But this is precisely the scenario Lupton warns about, since once we go down the path of doing nothing, we become accustomed to nothing until even our passion erodes.

Work is holy, and work is good. Knowing this changes our motivation for work, it releases our satisfaction in work, it permits extemporaneous joy through work, it alters our conception of work, and it gives us the basis for recovering the godly way in which our work is done!

Sometimes, it's true, work must be endured.[40] But mainly, **our work is to be enjoyed.**

Even so, I have noticed one thing, at least, that is
good. It is good for people to eat, drink, and
enjoy their work under the sun during the short life
God has given them, and to accept their lot in life.
And it is a good thing to receive wealth from God and
the good health to enjoy it. To enjoy your work
and accept your lot in life—this is indeed a gift from
God. God keeps such people so busy enjoying life
that they take no time to brood over the past.

Ecclesiastes 5:18–20

WHO SAYS WE HAVE TO BE ENOUGH?

$\diamond$ God placed humanity within a Garden temple and commanded Adam and Eve to fill the earth and subdue it.

Fill it . . . with what?

With people. Adam and Eve—whose names, to us, mean "The man" and "The female"—were meant to make more *adams* and more *eves*. God made the first humans capable of making the rest of the humans so people could go on doing the things God required. Adam and Eve didn't need to do their work alone. Creation would become the family business, the legacy of Eden, and the promise of cooperative work with God.

The world must have seemed so big, and Eden, comparatively, must have felt very small. Isn't that always the way? God overwhelms us with opportunity, with adventure, and with risk. We never feel like enough . . . because we aren't.

Who told us we need to be enough? Who deceived us into thinking that, unless we could do it all ourselves, we shouldn't even bother?

This is such a conundrum because the world and the work are ours. No one is coming to fix us or save us (not in this life!). No one will eat healthily for us. No one will exercise for us. No one will apologize for us or show mercy for us or reconcile with our brothers on our behalf. Our lives are entirely up to us. We cannot wait for someone else to solve our problems. And yet, we cannot do it all alone.

How are we to make sense of this? That we must do our part, and yet our part is deficient; that we must achieve all that God has placed within us to perform, and yet all such achievements are insufficient?

I'll tell you how.

It begins with understanding.

> Success is not elevation but satisfaction.
> Victory is not defeating your opponent but overcoming yourself.

> Your task is not to do everything nor to throw your hands up in resignation and do very little, but to perform all the Lord has placed within your heart until you are happily depleted and gloriously expired.

> > Live with love. Bless with tears. Die with scars.
> > Fill the world with altruism, self-sacrifice, and hope.

We do what's ours, trusting God to inspire others to do likewise. But we *must* do what's ours.

We are heirs of Eden. Our first tasks are our remaining tasks: create, define, collaborate, subdue chaos, invent understandings, revel in goodness, suppress dis-ease, overcome frailty, appreciate beauty, cultivate love, generate wholeness.

When John describes the New Jerusalem—God's future redeemed world—he depicts a City.

This City is the same "place" as Eden—the river of life and the tree of life make this clear—but it has also been expanded and cultivated into the City of God. Whereas Eden only took up a small piece of Earth's real estate, the New Jerusalem covers the whole earth.[41]

What began in a Garden ends in a Garden-City. The investment in Eden's children continues unbroken and divinely blessed.

Do you see what this means?

As we fill the Earth and subdue it, bringing dominion over the living members of Creation, we are civilizing the planet. "The ultimate goal set before humanity," says pastor-theologian Tim Keller, " . . . is that there should be an urban structuring of human historical existence."[42] **We are extending the borders of Eden** until this one hillock has grown to cover all continents, waterways, and boundaries; until everything is Edenic in the Garden-City of God. The perimeter of this Garden-City extends over the entire earth.[43]

God gave us an unfinished Creation, inviting us to cooperate with God in its completion.

We cannot cultivate this Garden paradise by ourselves. We need one another. Our relationships with other people are not merely good investments but divine contributions.

We help one another become more like God.

This has always been our task—to work with God and to work on the world. We were always meant to find ways to enjoy this work and to enjoy one another as we labor together, dreaming and manifesting all we can righteously conceive. Such trajectory gives our lives shape and meaning, allowing for course corrections whenever we go astray.

We must never fail to connect our origin to our destiny, and our destiny is to make a world we love.

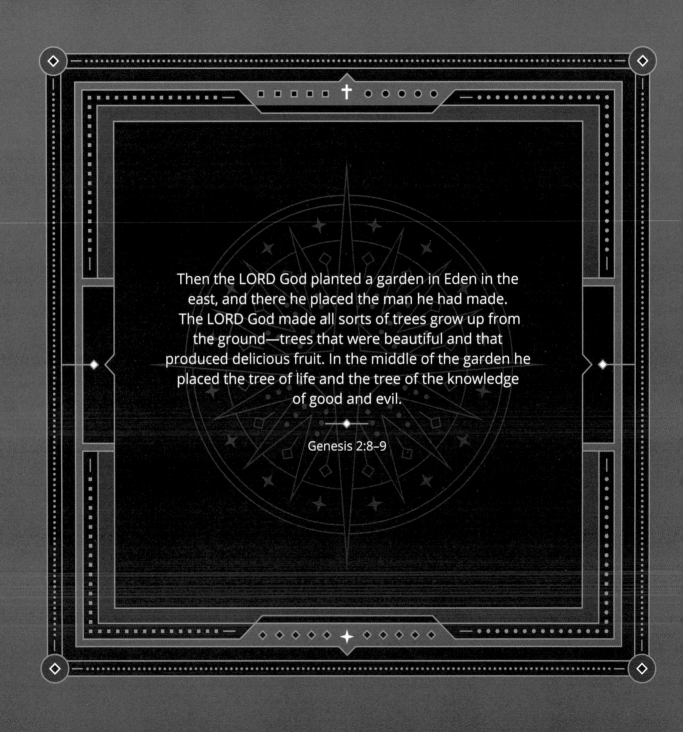

Then the LORD God planted a garden in Eden in the east, and there he placed the man he had made. The LORD God made all sorts of trees grow up from the ground—trees that were beautiful and that produced delicious fruit. In the middle of the garden he placed the tree of life and the tree of the knowledge of good and evil.

Genesis 2:8–9

7

WE ARE CALLED TO BRING
WISE ORDER TO CREATION

✦ Contemporary gardens differ from gardens in the ancient Near East.

Consider what we know about gardens in that time period, particularly in Mesopotamia. They were more like orchards and labyrinths than primeval forests. A garden had structure, boundaries, and design. Gardens were walled, cultivated, well ordered, and carefully landscaped, with a myriad of flowers and plants and trees, with rivers and pools and falls, and with aviaries and apiaries, requiring immense human investment, creativity, and ongoing care.

If we are to rightly imagine Eden as a "garden" in which Adam and Eve worked alongside God, then we must consider that Eden may have included buildings.[44] Even modern gardens often include trellises, arbors, gazebos, and pergolas. Medieval gardens included "follies," buildings with no real use other than to display the creativity of the architect and sometimes provide a better view for the upper class as they strolled through their well-developed playgrounds.

My point is that **our ancestors began cocreating immediately.** Eden wasn't just a few planter pots and some organic greens but the protology of the city—the beginning of human development and cultural emergence that would result in "agriculture, architecture, the arts, science, family life, business, and commerce, [that developed] a God-honoring civilization under God's reign."[45]

God entrusted us with the mandate to cultivate and develop the earth. We are called to draw together the resources of Creation, to bring wise order to the Garden, and to release human potential. Adam and Eve began doing so immediately, and you and I need to be reminded that's why we're here—not simply to live but to experience the best quality of life now and forevermore. We are meant to work alongside our Creator perpetuating Creation. That's how we get the world we want, and that's how we enjoy life as God intended.

The trick is to see how our work now not only recalls the work God mandated in the beginning but also anticipates the work God requires at the end. The Garden is merely our starting point. God looks excitedly to see what we will do with it. The divine-human partnership relies on our ingenuity, our imagination, and our industry. Once we realize this, then our work becomes prayer, sanctified by our inspiration and offered up to God as praise. How so? Because when we do anything "as unto the Lord," the outward behaviors don't necessarily change, but our intent does—our will changes, our heart changes, our orientation changes. Thus, something ordinary becomes infinite; something mundane becomes mysteriously holy.

Our work is glorified.

To be sure, most of us fail to appreciate how "going to work" is an act of glorification, but here it is critical to be reminded of the difference between a job and a vocation. Your job pays the bills, but your work—your holy calling, the internal wiring of God's Spirit that spurs

and prompts you to sacrifice sleep and talk excitedly at parties, the white-hot fire that burns in your belly when you recall all you intend to create—is the true reason for which you were made. Do your work and love it. Do your job and make the best of it. But whatever you do, in word or deed, for pay or for pleasure, do it as unto the Lord.

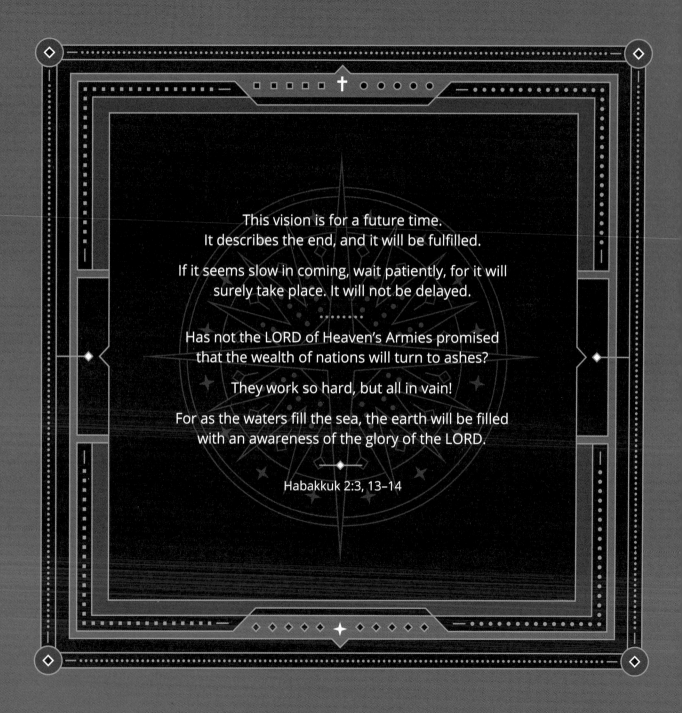

This vision is for a future time.
It describes the end, and it will be fulfilled.

If it seems slow in coming, wait patiently, for it will
surely take place. It will not be delayed.

⋯⋯⋯

Has not the LORD of Heaven's Armies promised
that the wealth of nations will turn to ashes?

They work so hard, but all in vain!

For as the waters fill the sea, the earth will be filled
with an awareness of the glory of the LORD.

———◆———

Habakkuk 2:3, 13–14

WE ARE CALLED TO DRAW TOGETHER
CREATION'S RESOURCES

There's a Jewish legend about a rabbi who was asked which was better: the things God made or the things we make. The rabbi knew the question was coming and had both hands behind his back, nodding thoughtfully at his questioner. When the time came to respond, the rabbi produced his hands. In one, he held an ear of corn; in the other, he held a cake. "God made one," he said, "and I made the other. Which would you rather eat?"

I'd rather eat cake. Wouldn't you?

In almost thirty years as a pastor, I've come across three major attitudes toward Creation. There are some who feel the earth belongs to God, and we should leave it alone. They perceive every industrial or societal activity as a cancer slowly killing our world, believing God made everything the way it was intended to be, and humanity's only contribution has been corruption.

There are others who believe the world is our playground, and we can do whatever we like. We are, after all, the dominant species on the planet. If the earth doesn't work for us, it

doesn't matter who else—trees, animals, insects—finds it habitable since we won't be around to care. These are the people who exploit natural resources for fast gains, often ignoring the long-term consequences of their activity.

Finally, there are those who believe we have a responsibility to work with the earth and bring out the best Creation has to offer for the maximum benefit of the world. These are the people for whom the triple bottom line of profit, people, planet is not just a byline but a conviction.

To summarize, either we should leave it alone, do stuff *to* it, or do stuff *with* it.

Of course, these categories are unfair. I've never met anyone who would admit to either of the first two options. But our actions often betray what we really believe, and many apparently think that God either did everything worth doing or did very little that helps us now.

Yet the best option is to realize **God made everything we need to make everything we need.** God gave us the raw materials we need to develop the world into a perfect habitat for growing humanity. God supplied enough food, water, soil, and clean air to sustain a population far greater than what we currently entertain. God gifted humanity with intelligence, reason, and curiosity enough to figure out how to move forward from the Garden to the City.[46]

We need to build, to enhance, to elaborate, to develop, and to cultivate. Somebody has to bring a bottle of wine to dinner if we're going to toast one another's successes, celebrate one another's company, and linger long after the table has been cleared.

After all, you can't have the Eucharist with a fistful of grapes.

Some wandered in the wilderness, lost
and homeless.

Hungry and thirsty, they nearly died.

"LORD, help!" they cried in their trouble, and he
rescued them from their distress.

He led them straight to safety, to a city where
they could live.

Let them praise the LORD for his great love
and for the wonderful things he has done for them.

For he satisfies the thirsty and fills
the hungry with good things.

———

Psalm 107:4–9

IMAGINATION, AGENCY, AND RELATIONSHIP

We're meant to pick up where God left off. And that's not to suggest that God has abandoned the project of Creation, only that all remaining work is cooperative.

The Creator created creators, bestowing us with imagination. But **God gave us more than just the ability to dream. God also granted us agency, meaning power and instrumentality to perpetuate Creation. We serve as God's vice-regents, working together as one human family in emulation of our Maker.**

I confess, some of these words are awkward—*agency*, for one, and *vice-regents*, for another—but they're the right words. They remind us we're connected to God—made by God to be like God—and also that we've been charged by God to do the things God does.

Remember, the Hebrew word for "image" (*tselem*) can also be rendered as "shadow." It means **when we're at work in the world, God's presence is felt and God's authority is remembered.**

These features of Edenic life—imagination, agency, and relationship—are enticing, but there is a danger of God's good things ironically distracting us from God. Yearning for God's things without God is like yearning for sex without another person. It's a sad kind of pleasure-seeking that makes God secondary to our desires.

So, all our creative work—whether that of fixing or making, the two chief creative pursuits in both business and art—is cooperative. We work with God to heal the world. We walk in the Spirit. We stay in step with the Word. For in Christ we live and move and have our being.

The heavens belong to the LORD, but he has given
the earth to all humanity.

The dead cannot sing praises to the LORD, for they
have gone into the silence of the grave.

But we can praise the LORD both now and forever!

Praise the LORD!

Psalm 115:16–18

WE INVENTED THE FUTURE

† God created the Garden, but we receive no indication that God created the means of taking care of Eden other than providing the first human family.

This means Adam and Eve would have had to invent *everything*.

It takes a special quality for someone to hypothesize turning a tree into a kayak or a stone into a kiln. It's another skill entirely for someone to actually do it. The first time someone stretched a string across an open box to make music must have felt like a miracle. But to craft complex stringed instruments, to arrange the composition of the music, and to appropriate that music for celebration, liturgy, and festival would have required incredible ingenuity.

And people did that. *We* did that.

We made it all, and we made it all up. We envisioned it all. We designed it all. We prototyped it all. We crafted it all. We improved upon it all. We use it all.

God made people, and people are amazing.

Genesis 4 and 5 give us a survey of the application of art, manufacturing, craftsmanship, science, and architecture through released human potential. Part of shadowing God then is the imaginative work of fixing and making, the creative application of competence to ideation.

The words *culture* and *cultivate* derive from the same root, *colere*, which means both "inhabit" and "tend."[47] We tend to that which lives in the ground, in ourselves, and in our world. We are cultured, and we create culture. This is what's so misplaced about the idea of a culture war. **We aren't meant to change culture, but to create it.** The more we invest in our God-given mandate to inhabit this world and flourish within it, the more the world will be transformed through acts of creative goodness.

God is first revealed to us as a Creator, and we are made by God to become like God. We are creators also, and we participate with our Creator in the ongoing work of Creation.

Our true humanity is godly.

But there is another element to all this creative work in Eden, one that gets to the foundation of why God created anything in the first place. Why does God want us to create? Because when we create, it brings God glory. **By expanding Eden, we allow others to come into close proximity with God's presence.** That, remember, is the key feature of both priests and idols in ancient temples—they mediate the presence and authority of their gods; likewise, as God's image-bearers living in God's earthly temple, people mediate the presence and authority of God. So, the untamed wilderness, now tamed, must acknowledge that it has been tamed by God's people working in God's way on God's tasks.

The more you create, the more you build. The more you grow and develop and work and love, the more glory God receives. We work for the Lord, and the Lord rejoices in our endeavors. As we work for God, God grows in us and God's presence and authority are more readily experienced through our efforts, stretching forward to a time when the earth is filled with the glory of the Lord like the waters cover the sea.

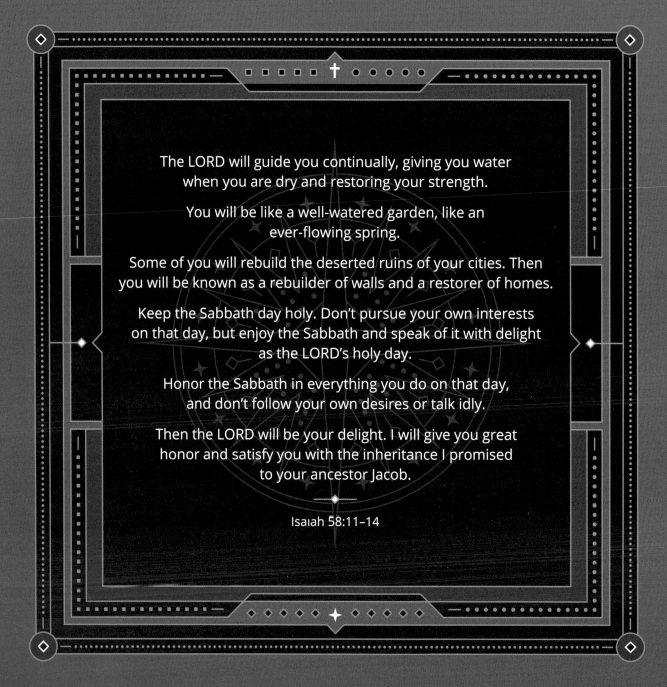

The LORD will guide you continually, giving you water
when you are dry and restoring your strength.

You will be like a well-watered garden, like an
ever-flowing spring.

Some of you will rebuild the deserted ruins of your cities. Then
you will be known as a rebuilder of walls and a restorer of homes.

Keep the Sabbath day holy. Don't pursue your own interests
on that day, but enjoy the Sabbath and speak of it with delight
as the LORD's holy day.

Honor the Sabbath in everything you do on that day,
and don't follow your own desires or talk idly.

Then the LORD will be your delight. I will give you great
honor and satisfy you with the inheritance I promised
to your ancestor Jacob.

Isaiah 58:11–14

EXPLORING EDEN

✧ Four is the number of the earth.

There are four corners of the earth[48], four cardinal points of the compass[49], four winds[50], four living creatures that patrol the heavens[51], and the fourth commandment concludes the creation of the material world[52].

Eden had four rivers running out of it[53], meaning they originated in the Garden. Rivers represent life and are teeming with fish, insects, and bacteria, to say nothing of their attractiveness to birds and mammals as a water source. These four rivers went forth from Eden, which means they were the delivery system for Edenic life. These rivers carried God's glory from the Garden to the rest of Creation. They were the means of export, taking God's idealized Life and pushing it to the rest of the world, an ecological counterpart to the goodness Adam and Eve were meant to export as they subdued the earth and won dominion over all that lived.

The key promise of Eden entails God giving God's people God's gameplan in God's place, resulting in God's blessing. That's what the four rivers signify—Edenic Life, exported over

the world.

That's what you and I are meant to perpetuate. We've been called to export Eden's goodness, to cover the earth with the knowledge of the glory of God. We're called to draw together the resources of Creation, to establish wise order, and to release human potential. That work takes many forms—trades, markets, agriculture, government—but all forms entail one specific requirement.

Dominion.

It's a strange word, isn't it? It feels like it belongs in a medieval fantasy. It's also a word that sounds suspiciously like domination. Sadly, too many people have operated as though they were synonyms. But dominion isn't domination. Dominion means the application of wise rule resulting in the optimal conditions for human flourishing.

I realize that sounds like a mouthful, and it is, so let me simplify. **Dominion means being wise enough to get the job done, willing enough to do the job well, and purposed enough to make sure the job doesn't do any unnecessary damage in the process.**

Exercising dominion means cultivating and caring for life. As my friend and mentor, Len Sweet, maintains, we are here to "conserve and conceive God's creativity, to tend and to till God's Garden."[54]

Tim Keller, pastor of Redeemer Presbyterian Church in Manhattan, compares the exercise of dominion to horticulture. Keller reminds us "a gardener neither leaves the ground as is, nor does he destroy it. Instead, he rearranges it to produce food and plants for human life."[55]

A dominator destroys anything in opposition to their will. But a person exercising dominion is not interested in the imposition of their will but in the ongoing flourishing and development of life.

Willfulness betrays a stubborn demand that the world comply to our desires, ambitions, and preferences. Willingness, on the other hand, refers to the humility inherent in receiving a task from God to do what God wants in the ways God wants to achieve the results God requires.

We have been given a mandate for dominion and willingly accept our responsibility before God to see the earth cultivated, cultured, and civilized. We have a good model for this kind of willing dominion in Jesus Christ. When the scripture speaks of Jesus having dominion,[56] they speak of his peace-inducing, world-healing governance.

Jesus is portrayed as a King in the Bible, but he's a funny kind of King. He's a King who refuses to send his armies to war,[57] he's a King who ensures the only casualty in any conflict is himself,[58] and he's a King who gives up all his power.[59]

At the end of the Bible, we read about God looking for someone who is worthy to open the scroll containing God's ultimate plan to heal the world,[60] No one is found worthy —not politicians or warriors or statesmen or teachers—except King Jesus, the Lamb That Was Slain.

And why is Jesus worthy? Why can he be entrusted to heal the world and restore the blueprint of Eden on a global scale? Because we know what Jesus does with power. Because we know what Jesus does with authority. Because we know what Jesus does with dominion.

When you and I do our noble work in the world, we've got to work like Christ. **We've got to accept our divine responsibility with the necessary humility to ensure that we bring forth the best, not only for humanity but from humanity as well.**

We are Eden's heirs exporting Eden's goodness, willingly working with God to exercise dominion over the earth for the glory of, and with the same spirit as, Jesus.

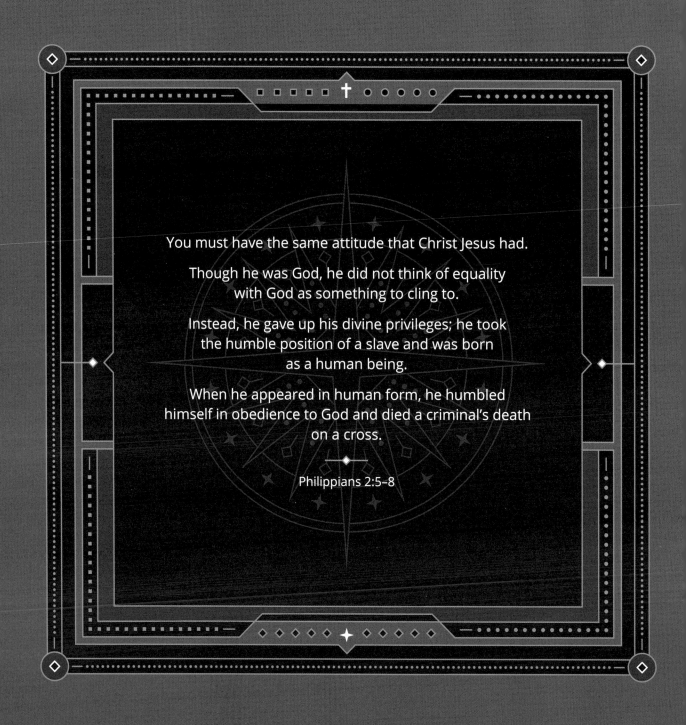

You must have the same attitude that Christ Jesus had.

Though he was God, he did not think of equality
with God as something to cling to.

Instead, he gave up his divine privileges; he took
the humble position of a slave and was born
as a human being.

When he appeared in human form, he humbled
himself in obedience to God and died a criminal's death
on a cross.

Philippians 2:5–8

WE ARE GOD'S

† We all crave meaningful connection. That's part of what it means to be human. We need togetherness. That's why we inflict road trips on our families, why we go to parties, and why we look forward to Thanksgiving.

We aren't meant to be alone.

There's nothing worse than feeling alone in the middle of a crowd. I think that's why so many of our social events hold such terror. We want to be with other people—really with them— but at the same time, we're frightened that we might get around other people and discover they don't really want to be with us.

In Eden, God gave Adam and Eve to each other. God supplied relationship.

At first, that sounds great. But if you've ever had a relationship, then you know they're not all they're cracked up to be. Relationships can be difficult. They can tire. Grow stale. Fracture. Wither. Even die.

Relationships by themselves are not enough. It may not be good for us to be alone, but it's awful to be stuck with someone you hate.

Thankfully, God didn't provide just relationship but agency—the ability to do things, to take action, to redress and repair and rebuild. To be an agent is to be the precise opposite of a patient. Patients have things done to them—doctors operate on patients, dentists fill cavities on patients, psychiatrists prescribe medication to patients. But agents do things of their own volition. To have agency means you have a choice. You don't have to just sit there. You don't have to take it. Not anymore. Not for one second. You don't have to let them speak to you like that, hurt you that way, or overlook your contribution. You don't have to wallow or hide or withdraw.

When God gave us relationship, God also gave us the means to heal that relationship when it splinters and to stimulate that relationship when it becomes lifeless. And in order that we might figure out what to do in those scenarios, God gifted us with imagination.

We can make things, and we can make things up. Whole worlds, even!

In Eden, **God gifted us with imagination, agency, and relationship.**

That connection doesn't just tether us to one another but also to God. After all, our relationship with God meanders in a similar fashion, and there will be times when we need to reinvigorate our devotion or rectify our brokenness. So, we repent. We try new disciplines. We learn from others. We delve more deeply into scripture. God gave us the ability to further our relationship with God.

We connect to God and, through God, to others. This sequence is critical. Whenever we strive for connection with others without first connecting to God, we neglect both our origin and our engine.

Our origin, meaning the people we were created to become.

Our engine, meaning God's Spirit within us, energizing our transformation.

We forget that **we are first God's.** Within such memory lapse, we find ourselves often at the mercy of other people's opinions, remarks, and reactions. If other people don't like us, we become insecure; if other people are unkind, we are wounded; if other people are intimidating, we become defensive and shy. But when we root ourselves in peace, in love, in God's mandate to perpetuate Creation—we remember all things are possible,[61] we are more than conquerors,[62] we are royalty,[63] possessing gifts[64] and insights and wisdom far beyond what we have earned.

We begin again with God.

The Lord is our refuge and our strength, our present help in times of trouble.[65] That's the ultimate connection, the ultimate gift of Eden—knowing we are never truly alone.

Our relationships with others are formed and funded by our relationship with God. We can love them because we recognize God's shadow upon them. We see God's law in their virtues, just as we see the requirement of God's grace evidenced by their flaws. God corrects our vision, removing the distortion of others, so we can see them as God sees them, as people worthy of dignity and love.

And in the end, we are free to love one another recklessly, passionately, and wholly.

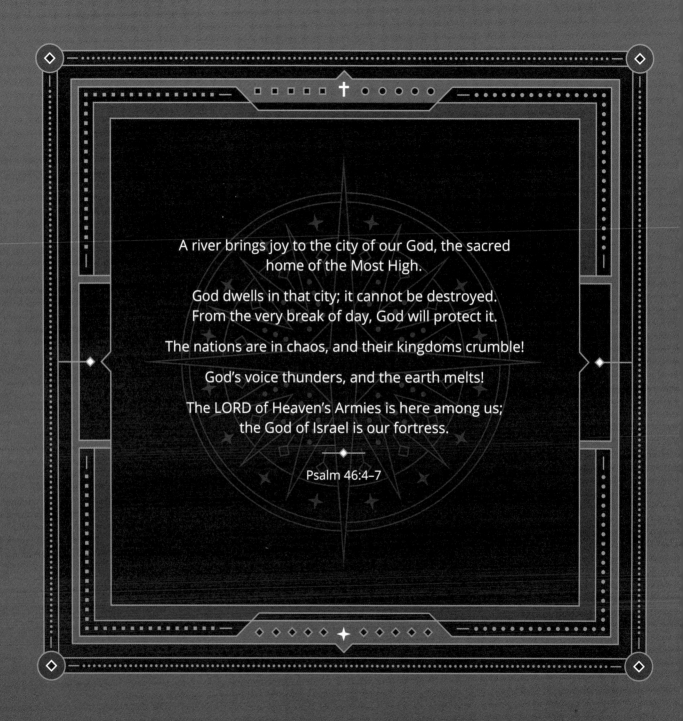

A river brings joy to the city of our God, the sacred
home of the Most High.

God dwells in that city; it cannot be destroyed.
From the very break of day, God will protect it.

The nations are in chaos, and their kingdoms crumble!

God's voice thunders, and the earth melts!

The LORD of Heaven's Armies is here among us;
the God of Israel is our fortress.

Psalm 46:4–7

GOD GAVE US A GARDEN
BUT REQUIRES FROM US A CITY

⚷ Reading through the Bible gives us a massive overview of God's long-term plans for divine human cooperation. The end of Revelation reveals that God's ultimate goal of working with humanity is a heavenly Garden-City.[66]

God gave us a Garden but requires from us a City. **The Garden was God's gift to us. The City is our gift to God, proof that we have done as intended.**

The Christian vision of the future isn't about us leaving earth to go to Heaven; it's about Heaven interpenetrating earth in New Creation.[67]

Our lives are fundamentally shaped by this future. We have a forward-looking faith, even while simultaneously having a historical faith. We need to continue along this trajectory, first begun in the Garden, carried on through the prophets, locked in by Jesus, honed by the apostles, and carried forward by the Holy Spirit in anticipation of God's glorified future.

And as we work toward this future, we begin to experience God's blessings. We experience abundance and prosperity as life's conditions, relationships, and holism are improved.

Why?

Because **when we do the things God wants and live the way God intends, not only do we give God glory but that glory overflows onto us.**

God designed us to live in an Edenic paradise, one that we're meant to expand across the entire world in cooperation with our Creator. Is there a better word for such a life than "blessed"? The goal of our lives is to glorify God, just as Saint Paul instructs in 1 Corinthians 10:31, "So whether you eat or drink, or whatever you do, do it all for the glory of God."

Our work is meant to bring God glory until that glory covers the earth.[68] This global glorification occurs as the boundaries of Eden are expanded and life on earth increasingly reflects life as it is in Heaven. **The more good work we do, the more other people will see our noble efforts and glorify God.**

We do good works because good works.

God's goal for us, and for the world, is glory—a life soaked in blessing, dripping in recognition that all blessings ultimately come from and reside in God.

As we fulfill our Edenic mandate to draw together resources, establish wise order, and release human potential, we cultivate the City of God all over the earth. And there is a residual benefit for obedience, stewardship, and creativity. Because when we live the way God wants, we experience life the way God intends, not only as a reward but as a result.

God is glorified through our work. God is glorified in our obedience. God is glorified in our blessing.

And that's precisely what God wants—glory! The Garden-City we are meant to create is valuable to God because God will live there with us.[69] God inhabits the praises of the people[70], and when we work for the Lord, all our work[71] becomes the dwelling place of our Creator. God is not merely pleased by our efforts but resides within them—now a little; later wholly and eternally.

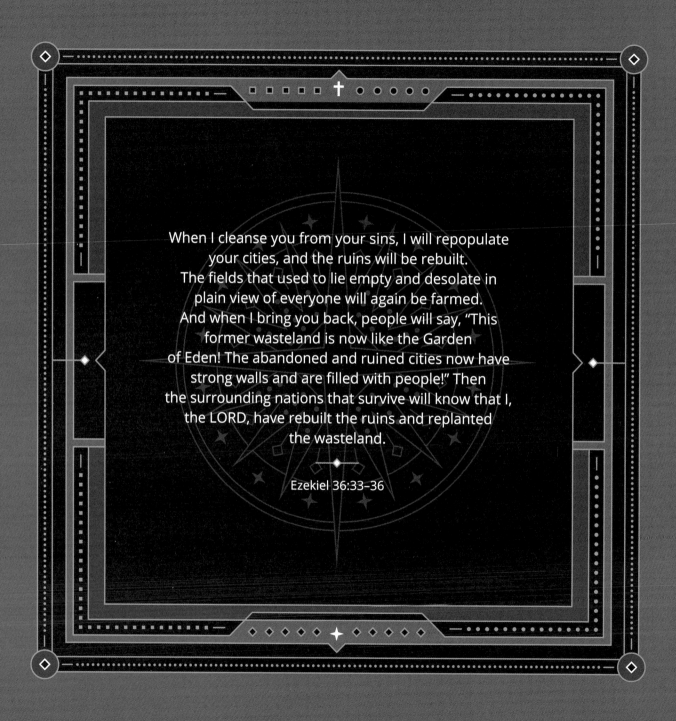

When I cleanse you from your sins, I will repopulate
your cities, and the ruins will be rebuilt.
The fields that used to lie empty and desolate in
plain view of everyone will again be farmed.
And when I bring you back, people will say, "This
former wasteland is now like the Garden
of Eden! The abandoned and ruined cities now have
strong walls and are filled with people!" Then
the surrounding nations that survive will know that I,
the LORD, have rebuilt the ruins and replanted
the wasteland.

Ezekiel 36:33–36

14

SOURCE AND DESTINATION

⚑ Have you ever been curious about Heaven? Snuck glimpses at the back of your Bible to see if you can decipher the hidden meanings in Revelation?

That's normal. Perhaps even healthy!

Connecting our origin to our destiny may be the single most neglected task of Christianity in the West.

Faced with an avalanche of weird ideas, pseudoprophecies, and outright speculative nonsense, most of us have given up any real hope of figuring out how God plans to set Creation to rights. The old adage claims we waste too much time on the "furniture in Heaven" and the "temperature in hell."

And yet . . .

I'm convinced our curiosity can serve us.

After all, don't our longings for the truth about Heaven ennoble us to live chastely, to act virtuously, and to guard our spirits against contamination? Doesn't our heavenly curiosity motivate us to study, to delve into the scriptures, and to prayerfully consider what we've learned?

The Jewish prophets foretold a time when all people would be filled with the Spirit of God.[72] In Revelation 21, then, we should not be surprised that God's glorious presence covers the whole earth. This is at least part of what John the Revelator intended when he described the City of God as a perfect cube,[73] reminiscent of the holy of holies.

A cube—think about that. It is perfect. It is equal in every direction. It holds everything. It has no gaps, no pores, and no inconsistencies. Everything fits. All Creation functions as God's sanctuary,[74] not just one portion of a secluded Eden. Everything will ultimately be expropriated for worship. Everything finds its ultimate fulfillment in God, with God, and before God. Which is to say everything belongs. Everyone has a place. Nothing and no one is ever out of place. Which is good news for the misfits and miscreants of the world.

There is healing for sickness,[75] death, the nations, and nature in God's presence.

God dwells as much on us as in us. God lives in us like I live in a small town. And the features of the New Jerusalem correspond to the features of the Christian life. The golden streets are lit paths of righteousness and providence. The gates that represent the apostles and the tribes also represent the boundaries of faith, defined by those who have come before us. The leaves of the Tree of Life, meant for healing the nations, indicate that the fruit of our lives will heal the world around us. The river of life flows from God, through us, to the world.[76]

The life we're promised for eternity is the life we've got now, only better. It's feasting and laughing and music and work without gluttony or stomachache, humiliation or mockery, exhaustion or futility. This is what John means when he tells us God makes all things new[77] (a very different promise than God making 'all new things'). God takes what already exists and

sweetens it, perfects it, and removes any strain or stain from it completely. Our relationships will be exonerated, our loves will be sanctified, our creative energies will be intensified and uninhibited by sickness or death or fatigue or ego.

Perhaps that is the fullest understanding of Christ as Alpha and Omega. Those words don't just mean "beginning" and "end." They mean "source" and "goal." What God began in the Garden will be completed in the Garden-City. **God made us and will complete us.** So, yes, let your heavenly curiosity lead you, so long as it leads you to virtue, virility, and maturity in Christ. Then you'll experience the reality of living on earth as it is in Heaven, now as then, with Christ not only as your beginning and end but as your middle also. **God set you on this path, the Spirit maintains your heading, and Christ will greet you when you arrive.**

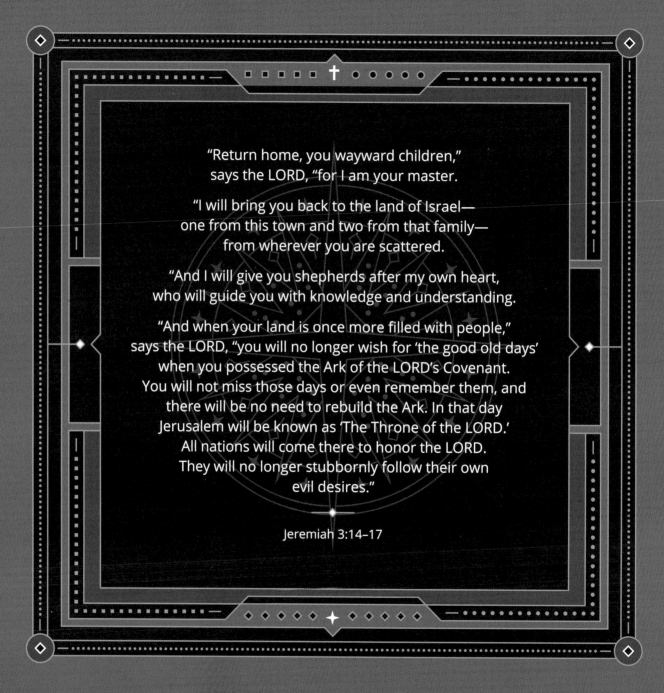

"Return home, you wayward children,"
says the LORD, "for I am your master.

"I will bring you back to the land of Israel—
one from this town and two from that family—
from wherever you are scattered.

"And I will give you shepherds after my own heart,
who will guide you with knowledge and understanding.

"And when your land is once more filled with people,"
says the LORD, "you will no longer wish for 'the good old days'
when you possessed the Ark of the LORD's Covenant.
You will not miss those days or even remember them, and
there will be no need to rebuild the Ark. In that day
Jerusalem will be known as 'The Throne of the LORD.'
All nations will come there to honor the LORD.
They will no longer stubbornly follow their own
evil desires."

Jeremiah 3:14–17

BORED WITH BLESSING

⚜ The first command in Eden was when the Lord God told us to "freely eat."[78] **Placed in a Garden-temple of inconceivable abundance, our first instructions were to enjoy Creation.**

Did we?

For how long?

How long did it take for us to tire of our good gifts from God?

How long does it ever take? Have we ever exhibited an ability to enjoy good things in perpetuity?

How long did it take for the Israelites to tire of manna and begin their complaint?[79]

How long did it take Judas to tire of following Jesus before he took matters into his own hands?[80]

How long does it take us to grow bored with the odyssey of obedience? How long before fidelity, ministry, and generosity feel like the same old, same old? How long before we wish to be our own gods?

Adam and Eve were placed as guardians in Eden, like warrior-priests set to sentinel the temple. But outside Eden, the world was untamed wilderness. Harsh. Ungoverned. And there were dangers beyond the Garden boundary, dangers for which humanity would always need to be prepared.

Our spiritual ancestors were meant to protect Eden, but they failed—intellectually, relationally, and teleologically. Paradise was lost, and we were expelled from Eden forever. We now live in a land of strife and violence, yet God has not rescinded the cultural mandate—we are still tasked with expanding the borders of Eden, though it's more difficult.

We lost Eden. Not only because we were disobedient but because we were ungrateful, inattentive, and bored.

You are amazing, and you have the power within you to make the world into something far more wonderful than it is. The reason you're sometimes bored is because you have not yet created all God has placed within you. You have not yet manifested your originality. You haven't built anything. You haven't yet achieved anything close to the scale of your competence. No one can be bored when they have a dream. No one can be bored when they're caught up in the fervor of actuating their noble ambitions to heal the world.

So, let's pay attention. Let's acknowledge the gifts God has given us. Invest ourselves in cooperative goodness. And repent of our boredom.

Then I saw a new heaven and a new earth, for the
old heaven and the old earth had disappeared.
And the sea was also gone. And I saw the holy city, the
new Jerusalem, coming down from God out of heaven
like a bride beautifully dressed for her husband.

I heard a loud shout from the throne, saying, "Look, God's
home is now among his people! He will live with them, and they
will be his people. God himself will be with them. He will wipe
every tear from their eyes, and there will be no more death or
sorrow or crying or pain. All these things are gone forever."

And the one sitting on the throne said, "Look, I am making
everything new!" And then he said to me, "Write this
down, for what I tell you is trustworthy and true." And he also
said, "It is finished! I am the Alpha and the Omega—the
Beginning and the End. To all who are thirsty I will give
freely from the springs of the water of life. All who are victorious
will inherit all these blessings, and I will be their God, and
they will be my children. . . ."

So he took me in the Spirit to a great, high mountain,
and he showed me the holy city, Jerusalem,
descending out of heaven from God. It shone with the glory
of God and sparkled like a precious stone—like jasper
as clear as crystal. The city wall was broad and high, with twelve
gates guarded by twelve angels. And the names of the
twelve tribes of Israel were written on the gates. . . .

I saw no temple in the city, for the Lord God Almighty and
the Lamb are its temple. And the city has no need of
sun or moon, for the glory of God illuminates the city, and the
Lamb is its light. The nations will walk in its light, and
the kings of the world will enter the city in all their glory. Its gates
will never be closed at the end of day because there
is no night there. And all the nations will bring their glory and
honor into the city. Nothing evil will be allowed
to enter, nor anyone who practices shameful idolatry and
dishonesty—but only those whose names are written
in the Lamb's Book of Life.

Revelation 21:1–7, 10–12, 22–27

✧ **W**e've spent most of our time exploring Eden, but now we'll journey through the scriptures, following people as they endeavor to fulfill the Creation mandate (however imperfectly). We'll continue using "the City" as shorthand for our work in the world, which includes drawing together the resources of Creation, bringing wise order to the world, and releasing human potential. We'll dive into some less familiar stories and characters as a means of better understanding ourselves and the many ways in which we flip back and forth between working with God and working against God and the many ways in which God dances around both our incompetence and our sin to prove that God's ultimate design for the Garden-City cannot, and will not, be disrupted.

BEGIN AGAIN (AGAIN)!

People who have never had to start over might idealize beginnings. But **beginnings are hard.** Starting over can be brutal. We don't have our social resources—our contacts, friends, support group. We might be without family, without familiarity, without a sense of who we are and what we've accomplished.

That was Cain's curse—to begin again, absent God.

After Adam and Eve were expelled from Eden, they had two sons, Cain and Abel. Abel picked up the mantle of God's work to perpetuate Creation, bringing forth the best of all he had.[81] Cain did not, opting instead to begrudgingly work as though he had been given a chore. Cain became jealous and killed his brother,[82] and for this he was sent east of Eden as a "homeless wanderer on the earth."[83]

In biblical literature, east is always the place of beginnings, and Cain is forever found in a place of beginning over and over again—wanting to get somewhere but unable to get anywhere because he makes his home in that beginning place. Beginning places are for leaving. They're where we're *from*.

Cain was stuck in a perpetual beginning, never arriving anywhere. Never getting ahead. Never achieving what he desired.

Have you ever felt like Cain? Adrift? Like you're condemned to a perpetual search for meaning, significance, and love?

In some sense, don't we always? Doesn't it feel like we're getting nowhere, despite working and trying and hoping and believing? Isn't there a voice in the back of our heads, accusing us of wasting our time, energy, and resources? Telling us we ought not to be so tolerant of others' mistakes, so patient with others' foibles, and so dismissive of our own greatness?

And what is the goal of this little voice? Our redemption? Our elevation?

No. The accusations come from the Accuser, who works against the purposes of God. Don't listen to the voice that compares you to Cain. You're not cut off. You have not been condemned. You have been justified,[84] adopted,[85] and called righteous by the only Judge who matters.[86]

Cain's home was the land of Nod, literally a place that is no-place, called "the land of wandering." It is less a place than the lack of a place, the opposite of Eden.

Cain turns his eye and his desire toward Eden, toward Paradise lost, ever mindful of the fact that he has forfeited the only thing that could bring him happiness: God's presence.

"He is therefore condemned to a perpetual searching for God's presence, the God with whom he wanted nothing to do and in whom he did not believe, and his very condition keeps him from ever finding [God]. Whatever he does, he cannot succeed, and that is the hopelessness of it all."[87]

You, however, ought to be brimming with hope. **You don't have to search for God; Christ has found you already.**

A single day in your courts is better than a
thousand anywhere else!

I would rather be a gatekeeper in the house of my God
than live the good life in the homes of the wicked.

For the LORD God is our sun and our shield.
He gives us grace and glory.

The LORD will withhold no good thing from those
who do what is right.

O LORD of Heaven's Armies, what joy for those
who trust in you.

Psalm 84:10–12

COUNTERFEITING GOD'S GAMEPLAN

$\dagger$ God made the world and entrusted it to us. God gave us a Garden but requires from us a City. God has always intended to work through people to draw together the resources of Creation, to bring wise order to the Garden, and to release human potential.

The world, and the work, is ours.

In the beginning, **God gave God's people God's gameplan in God's place, promising God's blessings.** But our spiritual ancestors deviated from that plan and were expelled from Eden. Their children fought, and Cain murdered his brother Abel. He was then cursed to wander.

Cain made his home in Nod, the land of wandering. There, he did two things: first, he took a wife, thereby creating a family; second, he founded the first human city, which he named after his son, Enoch.

Cain thought to reclaim Eden by doing what his father did, by fulfilling at least part of God's mandate from the Garden—*multiply!* Cain thought he could recover his divine calling by founding a city, but the security of that city was no substitute for the peace of the presence of God. And even though Cain was obedient in one sense, he still maintained his separation from God. That separation meant the city of Cain was in jeopardy from the very beginning.

Immediately after the city was founded, we read about the development of the arts in the musicianship of Jubal,[88] the tool-making of Tubal-cain,[89] and the creation of culture through architecture, agriculture, and technology.[90]

But in all these things, Cain tried to develop God's things without God. He absconded with God's gameplan for new people in no-place, achieving a counterfeit blessing.

We have tremendous power to create—culture, civilization, art, architecture . . . everything! But because our creative capacity is so remarkable, we often forget that our creativity is ultimately derivative. It comes from God. Our Creator created us to create. We were made. We were designed. And we were made by God to become like God. Consequently, when we disconnect our creativity from our Creator—when we attempt to employ God's gameplan without God—we find ourselves uprooted and adrift.

We create and build and manifest and achieve and wonder why all the things we create don't provide what they promise. Why doesn't wealth satisfy? Why doesn't achievement enduringly delight? Why doesn't the accumulation of pleasure intensify?

Could it be that we have sacrificed God's presence in pursuit of pleasure? These things—creativity, abundance, talent—are not evil in themselves (quite the contrary! We were made to experience these and so much more!), but absent God, these are like baubles with no Christmas tree, like rocks instead of stars, like coal that knows it was meant to be diamond.

That was Cain's real curse: he couldn't enjoy what he created while cut off from his Creator.

We have to learn from Cain's mistakes. God has placed within us the power to remake the world, but if we maintain our independence from God, then all our enjoyments and satisfactions will ultimately be aborted. God gave us a Garden and requires from us a City—but not just any city! God requires that we work together in the unfolding future of the New Jerusalem, that we constrain our creative pursuits to stay in step with the Spirit. Otherwise, our efforts will not produce Heaven on earth, but a counterfeit city like that of Cain.

In Hebrew, the city of Cain translates as "the Watching Angel, the Vengeance and Terror."[91] Clearly Cain's city isn't just a collection of houses but a spiritual power. As has often been said, we shape our cities, and then our cities shape us. Cain fled to the Land of Wandering, built a City of Terror in order to protect himself from untamed wilderness, and tried to fulfill God's gameplan without God, ever mindful of God's possible vengeance.

Cain could not escape God.

Though fractured, the Edenic image of God still resided within Cain, and he began to do the very things God desired in the Garden. Cain worked. Cain created. Cain sought refuge. Cain knew he had received dominion over Creation, but he seized it by force. He was the first Dominator, the first pervert of the divine calling. He imposed his will over Creation. He did things to Creation, taking what he wanted and spoiling what was left. Yet everything he found was fraud; everything he made was mistaken.

Cain spent his life in desperate search for security, "struggling against hostile forces, dominating men and nature, taking guarantees . . . that *appear* to him to be genuine, but which in fact protect him from nothing."[92]

There are too many Cains and too many who have been deceived into thinking that God's goods can be enjoyed without God's grace.

Don't let that happen to you. Do not believe the lie that your creativity, your work, or your achievements are rooted in your own cleverness. Everything you have comes from God, and to God everything must ultimately return. You can give it all to God as a gift or wait for God to reclaim it through adversity, disappointment, or loss.

The Lord gives, and the Lord takes away.

Blessed be the Name of the Lord.[93]

Unless the LORD builds a house, the work of the
builders is wasted.

Unless the LORD protects a city, guarding it
with sentries will do no good.

It is useless for you to work so hard from early morning
until late at night, anxiously working for food to eat;
for God gives rest to his loved ones.

Psalm 127:1–2

IDOLS AND ICONS

The greatest city in the ancient world was Ur, the birthplace of Abraham. Its 220 acres were filled with canals and harbors, gardens, markets, industry, and artistry. Ur demonstrated the potential in bringing together prosperity and power, peace and security. It was everywhere associated with "order, creation, civilization, life, and beauty."[94]

That's what people do. That's why God gave you the power to create, to manifest, to dream, and to build. From the very beginning of history, men and women like you have been astounding one another (and themselves) in service to the world. That's why we're here.

The world and the work is ours.

But we must always be careful. Once we release the potential within us, we must be careful to steward that energy. The lure of the City is always to glorify ourselves instead of our Creator, to poach God's glory.

Every person in every City is trying to make a name, either for themselves or for God. There's nothing wrong with being famous—just as there's nothing wrong with being wealthy,

influential, intelligent, or powerful—but there's an appropriate means of employing fame, as either an idol or an icon, a mirror or a reflector.[95]

An icon is like a convex mirror, showing people the reflection of God, giving God glory for every good thing; an idol is also like a mirror, but it's a flat mirror, only reflecting back the image of the person gazing into it.

Idols and icons are both mirrors, but the good news is that a mirror can be aimed by a human hand. Aim your life at the Lord. It's why you're here. It's why you were created. It's who you are. And every time you forget and get caught up in your own image, you're like a driver who gets caught staring in the rearview mirror instead of paying attention to the road ahead.

You're likely to crash.

Made in the image of our Creator, we all carry within us both the ability and the mandate to reflect God to the world. We are convex mirrors. When we're aimed truly, people look at us and are reminded of God's presence and authority. They see Christ in us. This is the impetus for colloquialisms like "You're the only Jesus the world will ever see" or "You are the hands and feet of Christ" or "You are an advertisement for God."

But most of us are not aimed true. At least some of the time, we're aiming our mirror right back at ourselves. We are self-obsessed. We stare at ourselves—both metaphorically and actually—and either overaccentuate our flaws or overcelebrate our attractiveness.

Even though our lives are good, they aren't meant to reflect our goodness. Our goodness is not sufficient to heal the world. This, ultimately, is what led Abraham to leave Ur and search for a city "designed and built by God."[96]

Wait—didn't God live in Ur? Doesn't God live everywhere?

Abraham's problem wasn't that God was absent, but that the people in Ur had designed a god of their own. After all, the most famous feature of Ur's enduring civic wonder was the ziggurat—a stepped temple rising above the alluvial plain. This tower-temple was called "the mountain of God"[97] and symbolized the relationship between that society and her deities, between heaven and earth, and between the people and the priesthood.

So, what was wrong with Ur?

In one sense, absolutely nothing. Ur sounds like the kind of City where most of us would desire to live. It had a stable infrastructure, fantastic amenities, and a vibrant spirit. Ur was a place where you could leave your mark on the world, where you could be exposed to new ideas and have your competencies stretched and your presuppositions challenged, where you could become a better version of yourself.

But Ur confused domination for dominion and conquest for cultivation. Like the City of Cain, Ur was trying to employ God's gameplan without God, hoping to counterfeit God's blessing. Ur was a place promising imagination, vocation, and connection while denying its Creator, mission, and presence.

Every City has the power to either direct or distract. **Cities can either help us flourish or make us famished, depending on the energizing power within.** There is darkness in the City, but light also.

The spirit of a City is the cumulative effect of the way people feel. Washington, DC, feels enthusiastically ambitious; Seattle feels futuristically convenient. It's easy to see how God cares about the spirit of a City, but God isn't trying to change the City itself. God wants to redeem and restore the people in it. The work of the City is achieved in the hearts of human beings, and the contest is being fought in the secret hopes of the young

Cities are desirable. Fashionable. Metropolitan. There's something alluring about living downtown, walking back and forth in the public square, being caught up in the energy of the crowds and the excitement of the urban thrum. And it's right for us to desire that energy. In fact, the desire we have for the density and diversity of downtown has been placed there by God.

God gave us a Garden, but God also gave us a yearning to turn that Garden into something more.

The City is the lure in our hearts, the dream of our cooperation with God. But we must never forget that dream came from God, is God's, and can only satisfy when we tailor our noble efforts to godly purpose.

Just as God made us to be creative and ingenious and powerful, God also made us to be in relationship with our Creator. We suffer when we are not.

We are icons, not idols.

We're here as missionaries, not tour guides; lifeguards, not beach bunnies; sherpas, not sightseers. We are here to work alongside God in the redemption and renewal of all things, to gather together Creation's resources, to bring wise order to the Garden, and to release human potential. With God's help. For God's glory. As soon as we neglect any component therein, we have lost our way and run the risk of attempting to institute God's gameplan without God. The result will be another Cain. Another Ur. Another Babel. Another ruin.

Sometimes we fall in love with our cities and become blind to the fact that they are in rebellion against God. People from New York claim God is pleased with their City because it is impressive; people from Los Angeles claim God is at work in their City because it is culturally significant; people from Vancouver claim God is evident in their City because it is ecologically

aware. I have yet to read any literature from people who acknowledge their cities are crummy, broken down, ramshackle excuses for civic centers yet love them anyway. Nobody ever speaks about loving their City because God has given them that city to love; no, they love their towns because they believe their towns are lovely.

Of course, we love San Francisco and Valletta and Berlin. Who wouldn't? That's not the issue. The issue of involvement in our earthly cities is whether we can bring the Light of Christ into a City enthralled by lesser lights.

Be wary of becoming a priest in a parody of peace that rejects God.

We must always strive to differentiate ourselves from the world, even as we labor lovingly within it. We must be the fulfillment of Habakkuk's prayer: "LORD, I have heard of your fame; I stand in awe of your deeds, LORD. Repeat them in our day, in our time make them known."[98]

We must be the ones to glorify God and acknowledge the beauty of Christ. Everyone else is too busy glorifying themselves.

When the people return to their homeland,
they will remove every trace of their vile images and
detestable idols. And I will give them singleness
of heart and put a new spirit within them. I will take
away their stony, stubborn heart and give them
a tender, responsive heart, so they will obey my decrees
and regulations. Then they will truly be my people,
and I will be their God.

Ezekiel 11:18–20

IF/THEN RELIGION

"'Canaan' came to be the cipher for the hierarchical urban polities along the fertile coastal plain. Each of these 'Canaanite' urban centers was dominated by a local god like Baal or Astarte or El, embodied in a local king."[99] People flocked to these City temples in hopes of procuring divine power and securing divine assistance. The basic relationship between an ancient City and her gods was the manipulation of supernatural power.

We call this "magic."

Sometimes magic involved the aid of the elements, sometimes the assistance of supernatural creatures, and sometimes the invocation of cosmic laws and universal powers.

The gods offered protection in exchange for praise.

Whether it's some deity from a pagan pantheon or some contemporary idol like money or sex or power, people often fail to realize that the relationship between themselves and their gods is always reciprocal. They *do something* in hopes of *getting something*.

Only with Christ is that relationship changed from reciprocity to grace. He gives us himself and all that comes with him because he loves us. That's it. We haven't earned it. We don't deserve it. God enriches us as human children because our God is a loving Father, not because we are especially pleasant.

The benefits of knowing Jesus often spill over into blessings, but I'm convinced those blessings are more result than reward. God instructs us to love our neighbor, and thus our relationships with our neighbors improve. But—and this is key—the Lord does not compel our neighbors to enjoy our company. The Lord does not make them do anything for us. The Lord doesn't control them, as though they were puppets made of meat. God simply knows how people work and how people work best together, and so instructs us in wisdom and knowledge, so we can benefit others as well as ourselves.

The truth is that most people—including Christians!—have a consumer's relationship with the invisible powers of this world. We try to buy everything and are disappointed when we learn there are some things for which we cannot barter. We're angry when we realize some circumstances cannot be improved just because we want them to be or because they're more favorable or because we're nice or because we've behaved well.

Any spirituality that promises an "if/then" blessing will be exposed as bankrupt. Our worship of things or fame or false gods can only disappoint. We may remain poor, unknown, and unfulfilled. Our relationship with the true God cannot make us rich, loved, and full of meaning while we persist in holding onto a bargain God never made.

To differentiate, prayer is petition; magic is compulsion. God responds to prayer by making us more like God, thereby increasing our understanding, our strength and resolve, and our serenity in the midst of tragedy; yet God never condescends to be compelled. God will not be controlled. No matter how perfectly you pray (as if there is such a thing as a perfect prayer!), **God will not do what you want.**

Our task is to live in line with God's desires, not the other way around.

Both Eden and Revelation expose pagan theology as a poor imitation of the divine-human relationship. There are many dangers in magic but none so hostile to the magician as herself.

In Eden, God walked among us,[100] with us, before us, and behind us. God's presence saturated the Garden without any intermediary. The Lord gave us protection without petition, and God's authority spurred us to expand the borders of Eden and spread glory over the earth.[101]

But we're not in Eden anymore, and it's easy to see why our ancestors built cities to imitate the perfection they had lost. Their imitations confused crucial details however. That's why in Revelation John goes to great lengths to show us there is no temple in Heaven.[102] Heaven, when it comes to earth, becomes the temple. God's presence once more saturates Creation. But instead of being centralized in a Garden, God's presence now spreads over the whole earth.[103] And the image of God within us that was once corrupted is not only restored but glorified.[104] We become new people with God's presence radiating inside us and altering us entirely.

That's our future, our ultimate destiny. That's the endpoint to which we are constantly traveling. We live in the time between times, between the Garden and the City, and everything we do pulls us closer to God's promised future.

God isn't interested in our spiritual purchasing power. God is not going to dominate the will of others because we've been tithing. God is not going to disrupt the character of others because we've begun to feel victimized. We think we'll give something to God in order to get something from God, but we have nothing to give that will force God to act contrary to divine nature. **God has already given us everything we need, and until we embrace and accept the divine character fully, we'll continue looking for handouts.**

Don't be deceived: the Christian life is not magic but grace. We don't convince God to do what we want. We invite God to re-form us into holier people, the best possible version of ourselves with God's help for God's glory.

You have come to mount Zion, to the city of the living God, the heavenly Jerusalem, and to countless thousands of angels in a joyful gathering. You have come to the assembly of God's firstborn children, whose names are written in heaven. You have come to God himself, who is the judge over all things. You have come to the spirits of the righteous ones in heaven who have now been made perfect. You have come to Jesus.

Hebrews 12:22–24a

GOD LOVES THE WORLD

The cities of refuge were the first cities God consecrated. There were plenty of cities by this point in human history,[105] and forty-eight Israelite cities were governed by the tribe of Levi, the priestly caste in ancient Israel. Of those Levitical cities, six were set aside as places of asylum,[106] so that if you were accused of a crime you could flee to these cities and be guaranteed a fair trial and protection from violent retribution at the hands of the avenger of blood.[107]

The cities of refuge demonstrate a remarkable strategy. Knowing that we had strayed from our original calling to expand the borders of Eden and knowing also that even God's own people were following more closely to the legacy of Cain—employing God's gameplan of human development without God's government, God's creativity, and God's peace—God decided not to wait for us to get back on track with the divine City; God would enter ours.

I love that!

God doesn't wait for us to return to our senses. God crafted humanity to enjoy us, to know us, and to cooperate with us in the work of the world. When we stray, God pursues. When we fail, God endures. When we quit, God redeems.

French theologian Jacques Ellul claims "God enters into the very heart of revolt and refusal,"[108] refurbishing these human cities as symbols of peace, justice, and divine protection.

That's who God is. That's how God works. God doesn't abandon broken cities, broken things, or broken people. **God doesn't build new cities but enters existing ones.** God sanctified those cities of refuge, taking something unholy and making it holy.

No matter how far we drift, no matter how fast we run, no matter how defiantly we shake our fists and demand we live our own truth, God shows up—unexpectedly, unobtrusively—and loves us. God loves our messes, and God loves to help us clean them up. God loves our mistakes and loves to show us they are not fatal. God loves our fierce demonstrations of personal prowess and loves to expose our weaknesses and then build us back into holier people.

And why? Why does God love all this, despite all our recklessness?

Because God so loved the world . . .

Throughout the Bible we see that God's orientation toward the world is love. God gives life to the world[109], coming not to condemn the world[110] but to save it.[111]

As Michael Mayne, Dean of Westminster, writes, "God blesses everything He creates, making all creation the sign of His presence. If spirituality means the way we grow into the kind of being we are intended to be, then the starting point is not a striving after another world, but a deepening awareness of the true nature of this world and our place in it."[112]

We must be involved in the redemption of all creation, "deepest heaven, everything on planet earth."[113]

The former Archbishop of Canterbury, William Temple, once warned us that "it is a mistake to think that God is only, or even chiefly, concerned with religion."[114]

What else does God care about? Might I be so bold as to suggest that God cares for *everything*? God values people, but not just people; and not just animals and plants or ecology either; but also cultures, societies, language, art, and technology. If "the earth is the LORD's, and everything in it," then surely we must begin to understand that God's interests uphold the sacred nature of all that is.

Christian spirituality contends for the redemption of the earth and all its contents. We uphold the mandate to revalue the world and hasten the day when greed and consumerism are exposed, when arrogance and irreverence are unplugged, when hurry and selfishness are repented of, and when the sacred-secular rift in our thinking is healed. We must not merely ascribe to such faith but take an active role in redemption. Like our Creator, we must enter the world and transform it rather than hoping that our good thoughts and smiles contribute to lasting change.

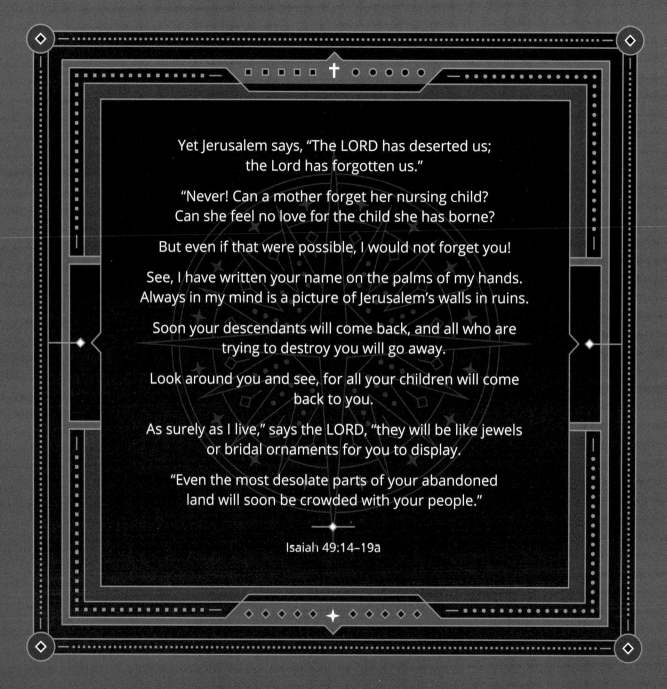

Yet Jerusalem says, "The LORD has deserted us;
the Lord has forgotten us."

"Never! Can a mother forget her nursing child?
Can she feel no love for the child she has borne?

But even if that were possible, I would not forget you!

See, I have written your name on the palms of my hands.
Always in my mind is a picture of Jerusalem's walls in ruins.

Soon your descendants will come back, and all who are
trying to destroy you will go away.

Look around you and see, for all your children will come
back to you.

As surely as I live," says the LORD, "they will be like jewels
or bridal ornaments for you to display.

"Even the most desolate parts of your abandoned
land will soon be crowded with your people."

Isaiah 49:14–19a

KISS OR KILL

† Jonathan Sacks, the Chief Rabbi of the United Hebrew congregations, says, "Where *what I can do* meets *what needs to be done*—there is God's challenge and our task."[115] That's how we must see the world. That's how we must live. Our lives are no accident. **God incubated us. God grew us. For this.**

The ideas we have—to beautify the world, to improve the world, to heal the world, to develop the world—and the resources to which we have access (networks, money, relationships, intellect, etc.) have all been granted by God in order that we might continue to cooperate with God as Eden's heirs.

The world and the work is ours.

God gave us a Garden but requires from us a City.

Every City has a *detritus* and an *aspiritus*, a worst-case scenario comprised of a city's cultural debris and a noble ambition within a city to be something better. Both *detritus* and *aspiritus* receive their energy from people. Lazy, unproductive naysayers produce negative energy that accelerates the City's *detritus*—its worst flaws magnified, left unchecked, and even glorified. Eager, committed, imaginative people produce positive energy that accelerates the City's *aspiritus*—noble ambitions, leading the City to become the best possible version of itself. This healthy spirit results in improved infrastructure and amenities, better offerings to both residents and visitors alike.

This isn't just true for large cities but also for small towns, churches, high schools, or even sports clubs. The way we speak about ourselves—our homes, our neighborhoods, our town centers—either elevates or denigrates them, each comment taking us a step closer toward the *detritus* or the *aspiritus*.

We kiss or we kill with every word.

The investments we make in our own cities are eternal investments in the City of God amid the cities of man. "God's city is different from human cities (like Babel) where skyscrapers are designed for their builders' own prosperity and prominence. . . . The city's cultural riches are produced, not for the glory of the producers, but for the joy of the entire earth and the honor of God."[116]

My prayer is that the investments each of us makes in the City return as dividends in our spirits. God's work always results in God's blessing, such that meaning follows obedience and satisfaction from stewardship.

When we live the way God wants, we get to enjoy life the way God intends. I stand by that statement, even while recognizing that it seems to promise blessing and peace more directly than we typically experience. But the truth is, God's gameplan results in God's blessing, and if we're ever going to experience Heaven—either here, in part, or later on, as a

whole—then we've got to realize there is a residual benefit for obedience, stewardship, and creativity.

Ultimately, there will always be two competing authorities in every place: the Rule of God—where imagination, vocation, and connection direct glory to God—and the Laws of Man—where man's work is subservient to man's fame, and the best we can hope for is to keep people from ruining one another. **Our task is to restore the broken order in the world, to live under the Rule of God while working within the Laws of Man.**

We have a lot of work to do, for we are God's response to evil, to poverty, and to injustice. What else could it possibly mean for us to be the body of Christ[117] than that our hands are God's hands and our minds bear God's thoughts?

We wonder why God hasn't done anything to arrest evil. But God has performed the most spectacular feat imaginable: God sent you!

Why is there injustice in the world? Why do bad things continue to happen?

Because you haven't stopped them yet. Because people like you have not yet risen up against the tyrants and the oppressors, against the warmongers and the pedophiles, against the profiteers and the traffickers. The world is ours. The only people who can fix it are those acting upon these words.

> You have been waiting for God, while God has been waiting for you. No wonder nothing is happening. You want God's intervention . . . while God wants your collaboration. *God's kingdom is here, but only insofar as you accept it, enter it, live it, and thereby establish it.*[118]

If you want evil to stop, then stop it. If you want injustice to end, then end it. Do not lament the ills of contemporary society. Resolve them.

There will always be people who disrupt goodness, but we must work, day by day, act by act, to achieve "a *redemption of small steps*."[119]

Whenever we repair some small part of the world, we repair ourselves.

We must wed our intentions to our activities. We must become the answer to our prayers.

Then I will praise God's name with singing,
and I will honor him with thanksgiving.

· · · · · · · ·

The humble will see their God at work and be glad.
Let all who seek God's help be encouraged.

For the LORD hears the cries of the needy; he does not
despise his imprisoned people.

Praise him, O heaven and earth, the seas and all that
move in them.

For God will save Jerusalem and rebuild the towns of Judah.

His people will live there and settle in their own land.

The descendants of those who obey him will inherit the land,
and those who love him will live there in safety.

——◆——

Psalm 69:30, 32–36

THE BEST POSSIBLE VERSION
OF OURSELVES

✦ Ever wonder why Heaven has paved roads?[120]

We don't know what means of transportation there will be in Heaven, whether cloud cars or high-speed public cherubim, but for there to be roads, and for those roads to be paved, means God has given some thought to how the City is laid out, to the ways traffic flows, and to the means by which people are meant to get around.

God has a plan, and those plans are paved in gold.

And those gold-paved plans indicate God intends people to move, to come together, and to pull apart. To cross-pollinate. To be active. We are not static but kinetic. Even in eternity, we will be going places. We will have people to see and things to do.

I have several friends who are convinced the great spiritual dis-ease of our time is busyness. They preach about the dangers of too much coming and going, too little downtime, insufficient boundaries, and a failure to simply "be."

They're right.

(Sort of.)

But the problem is not our activity. The problem is our panicky need to be better than everyone else, keep up with everyone else, show everyone else how capable and cosmopolitan and cool we are. And of course there are some who are not driven by comparison but by their master. When you work for Pharaoh, he demands more than you can reasonably give. You'll be exhausted and depleted because your work is soulless and banal. Even good work can hurt you if it's performed from an empty stage to a restless and dis-eased audience. So take care of yourself. And remember, it's not about your job or your paycheck but about passion and drive.

The solution, then, is not less activity but less exhibition and/or less exhaustion.

Follow the voice of the Spirit inside you, inside of the people around you.

Busyness may be the enemy, but activity most certainly is not. Otherwise, Heaven would have crystal hammocks and recliners carved from lapis lazuli.

And just like Heaven has some infrastructure, God intends for you and me to bring wise order to the world now, on earth as it is in heaven.

Infrastructure gives shape and power to humanity's efforts, thus doing the original work God mandated of drawing together the resources of Creation, bringing wise order to the Garden, and releasing human potential. We know that the work of developing and expanding Eden into its metropolitan counterpart is a decidedly human task. That's why **cities function as engines of human flourishing.** They drive us together and they drive us faster forward. They put us in contact with new and different people, diverse and varied cultures, and novel and exciting opportunities. Cities are competitive arenas that place us near others who are smarter than we are, more skilled than we are, and more ambitious than we are.

Cities force us to become better versions of ourselves.

That doesn't mean we need to compare ourselves to others or to pander for their approval. No—there is a healthy way in which people can spur one another on in acts of creative goodness, a healthy means of iron sharpening iron. For those who love life, it is easy to understand that when others live more than you, you want to get caught up in their current. You want to move faster. You want to see more. To do more. To live more. Not because you want to be like them but because you want to be more of yourself.

I know not everyone experiences this. Some find the fast pace of urban living wearying, perhaps even diametrically opposed to the way of the Spirit. Respectfully, I disagree. The long-term plans of our Creator, indeed the Edenic longing within ourselves, pulls us toward something more City-like than meadow-like. Some prefer a slower pace, and there's nothing wrong with that, but there are already innumerable books in praise of slowness. Spiritual pedestrianism dominates our bookstores and coffee houses, seminaries and seminars. The monkish and contemplative manifestations of spirituality are so ingrained into our consciousness that most find it difficult to consider any alternative without somehow compromising our fidelity, our Biblicism, or our virtue.

I contend there's more than one way to be spiritual. I believe the scriptures demonstrate the virtues of both the active and the contemplative life, the *vita activa* and *vita contemplativa*.

After all, what would the great contemplatives say to the Apostle Paul, who labored ceaselessly, sometimes even burning bridges between friends for the sake of the gospel? What would they say to King David or his son Solomon—whose artistic ambitions meant they were veritable powerhouses of creative output (all while governing a large and burgeoning kingdom)? What counsel would our modern sages of slowness give Ezekiel while he used his

body to perform prophetic declarations 24/7 for several years without rest? And what would they say to Jesus, who set aside his family, shouted and danced and drank too much, hung out with the wrong people, broke taboos, and went off by himself only a handful of times to pray?[121]

When we examine the scriptures as they were delivered to us, we realize there's as much profit in *accelerando* as *rubato*, as much merit in going a thousand miles with your hair on fire as slowly walking with owls, as much virtue in staying up all night and howling at the moon in impassioned madness as kneeling in your cloister watching the candle burn.

Perhaps this is difficult to accept. Please acknowledge that for some, this is good news! For some, it is a relief not to be burdened with the contemplative path.

The person who gets to determine what's healthiest for you is you. You are the one who knows how you're wired. You are the one with an understanding of your spiritual gifts. You're the one hearing the voice of the Spirit, following the promptings of God, and learning from those around you. And when you find yourself surrounded by other people who break the mold you've been told you have to fit (even though you clearly don't) and who love the Lord and love the world (you know, like Christ) and who want to soar with the eagles and run with the horses and climb mountains and ascend the hill of the Lord . . . what else can you do but rejoice?

Who knew we could be holy *like this*?

You did. You always knew. You just needed to be around other people who spurred you on instead of holding you back or declaring you were doing it wrong because you weren't doing it like everybody else.

Cities surround us with other people, such that we find other people like us, who are wired like us, who can show us how to be more fully ourselves while we simultaneously pursue God. When we see how they do it, and we realize there are many ways to be spiritual—rather than just the *vita contemplativa*—then we are inspired to find our own way forward in service to Christ.

Many have bemoaned my love for these fast-paced, enthusiastic, and sometimes competitive environments, but we shouldn't overlook the fact that if we're allowed to coast, we won't ever find true meaning or satisfaction in our work. We need other people to push us, to encourage us, and to demonstrate for us what can actually be done.

When we gather a collection of highly competitive people, we are not only fueling the engines of personal development but also multiplying those engines. It's not just about getting one or two people to put their best foot forward but about seeing what happens when their combined horsepower is unleashed on shared projects, with shared vision, telling the stories of our community.

We can go further together.

We are faster when we race.

The further we go and the faster we move starts to feel like training, like we're running to win a prize.[122] A victor's crown.[123] A life fully alive.[124] Abundant life.[125]

Don't you realize that in a race everyone runs, but only one person gets the prize? So run to win! All athletes are disciplined in their training. They do it to win a prize that will fade away, but we do it for an eternal prize. So I run with purpose in every step. I am not just shadowboxing. I discipline my body like an athlete, training it to do what it should. Otherwise, I fear that after preaching to others I myself might be disqualified.

1 Corinthians 9:24–27

WE ARE AMPLIFIERS

There's a substantial difference between playing guitar by the campfire and playing on stage in front of a crowd. The difference isn't just in song selection or talent, synergy or composition, but in a combination of factors that begin with amplification.

For example, if you have a singer and an acoustic guitar performing together, they can adjust to each other easily. But if you add a grand piano, it will now require a much higher degree of control to get the balance correct among the three instruments. Just hearing the vocals over the piano will be a challenge, and once you throw in a drum set, the game changes exponentially.

Whenever we gather together there is a natural swell in volume and intensity. At some point, that swell will outpace our individual ability to compensate, and we will need amplification. Amplification is any kind of artificial boost to ensure the instruments can be heard. Guitars have amplifiers, but nowadays most bands will even have dedicated amplifiers to mix their drums and percussion.

The work we do as Christians functions as an amplifier. We bring people together, draw them in, and make them feel like they're being heard, like they have a voice.

At some point, we must all realize we don't need to be the loudest voice in the room. There's a time to speak and a time to stay silent. There's a time to listen and a time to amplify. There are people who need to be heard, and we can use our power to give them a voice, a platform, and an audience. We can lend them our credibility and our network. We can point to them, gaining empathy for their cause—be it charitable, civil, or creative.

Somewhere, we've lost our willingness to amplify others. Even in the case of social justice, these days we're most interested in shouting loudest about injustice than in guaranteeing the least, the lost, the last, and the lonely are themselves heard. After all, there's a big difference between decrying our opponents for their selfishness and sharing the platform with someone who needs to tell their own story in their own voice in order to be validated, dignified, and known.

When we set our own voice aside and use the power we have to elevate others, we can reduce the vehemence of the us-and-them divide. We can give others the opportunity to help, to hear, and to heal. In that moment, instead of reminding our opponents how badly they've behaved in the past, we give them the chance to be better than they were.

We need to get ourselves in balance, lowering our own volume when it's not our turn to solo.

That's a critical component of healing the world. After all, making the world a better place doesn't necessarily involve making the world more like you—or me, or even us—but recognizing that we are one human family and that we need to care for one another if we're going to survive. Sometimes we will have insights into how things must move forward into God's promised future, but other times you and I must be committed to the work of searching out and hearing disparate voices that expose our blind spots, reveal our ignorance, and shore up our understanding about how the gospel manifests.

We're all part of one great body but with many parts. We need each other to function holistically. The parts of the body that are more vulnerable need greater protection. They need the stronger parts of the body to advocate for them, to cover them, and when appropriate, to ensure they get to perform.

The human body has many parts, but the many parts make up one whole body. So it is with the body of Christ. Some of us are Jews, some are Gentiles, some are slaves, and some are free. But we have all been baptized into one body by one Spirit, and we all share the same Spirit.

Yes, the body has many different parts, not just one part. If the foot says, "I am not a part of the body because I am not a hand," that does not make it any less a part of the body. And if the ear says, "I am not part of the body because I am not an eye," would that make it any less a part of the body? If the whole body were an eye, how would you hear? Or if your whole body were an ear, how would you smell anything?

But our bodies have many parts, and God has put
each part just where he wants it. How strange
a body would be if it had only one part! Yes, there are
many parts, but only one body. The eye can never
say to the hand, "I don't need you." The head can't say to
the feet, "I don't need you."

In fact, some parts of the body that seem weakest and least
important are actually the most necessary. And the
parts we regard as less honorable are those we clothe with the
greatest care. So we carefully protect those parts that
should not be seen, while the more honorable parts do not
require this special care. So God has put the body
together such that extra honor and care are given to those
parts that have less dignity. This makes for harmony
among the members, so that all the members care for each
other. If one part suffers, all the parts suffer with it,
and if one part is honored, all the parts are glad.

1 Corinthians 12:12–26

THE PRESENT IS PROPHETIC

In the middle of it all—going to work and going to church, looking after one another and chasing our dreams, working out and working on our goals—we sometimes wonder if what we're actually doing bears any similarity to what we're supposed to be doing. We wonder if God is at all pleased with our efforts. We wonder if our work matters, to God or anybody else, and whether it will last.

Eden is so far removed we can't even remember what it looked like. Heaven is so far forward we're not even sure it's there.

Are we getting closer to God? Or are we just preoccupied?

<sigh>

Be patient.

Despite the fact that our work with God fulfills a high and holy calling, it often looks like the tangles on the underside of a rug. God is weaving the rug, but we look like a mess. **The good**

news is that our work itself is redeemed, not just our souls. God sanctifies what we do when we do it for the Lord, and our work now anticipates God's finishing work in eternity.

I heard a parable once that exemplifies this nicely. Suppose a child builds a sandcastle on the beach. Will that sandcastle exist in eternity? Perhaps. Perhaps God is so charmed by the sandcastle that God ensures it never washes away, and so the child's work becomes eternal. Or perhaps God is so charmed, the child's work enlarges, and the original becomes a blueprint of sorts for an actual castle made of sand. The child can then visit and inhabit his work forever. Or perhaps in eternity the child has capacity to make for himself a thousand sand castles that will not wash away with the tide but instead live amphibiously. Who knows? It's a mystery. But the mystery is not whether our work will endure, but how. Perhaps, in all the ways I've illustrated. Perhaps in many, many more.

I like to imagine eternity as a never-ending occupation of the world we already inhabit. Perhaps it takes us the first few thousand years to dig up all our roads and undo the damage we've caused through our environmental disregard; perhaps, in eternity, we do not build homes out of lumber, but grow them by bending trees using techniques like baubotanik, tree sculpture, and arbortecture; perhaps it takes longer to heal the ozone layer or migrate to the sea. The point is that God doesn't make all new things, but all things new[126]—and God intends for us to be involved. We rule.[127] We reign.[128] We sing.[129] We judge.[130] We bear witness.[131] We eat.[132] We love.[133] There's nothing new under the sun[134], and there's nothing new once we no longer need the sun itself.[135] It's just us, better and improved, and God—the same yesterday, today, and forever.[136]

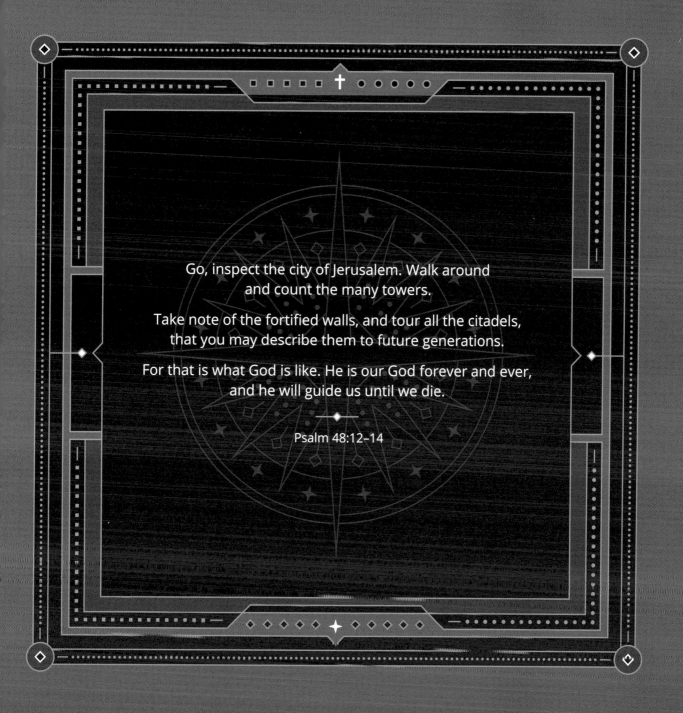

Go, inspect the city of Jerusalem. Walk around
and count the many towers.

Take note of the fortified walls, and tour all the citadels,
that you may describe them to future generations.

For that is what God is like. He is our God forever and ever,
and he will guide us until we die.

Psalm 48:12–14

COOPERATIVE WORK WITH GOD

One of my favorite writers is Wendell Berry. He's a poet and a conservationist, an old-school farmer with a love for the earth. Berry often speaks of his need to observe what the land is saying and to interfere as little as possible with the natural order: "The care of the earth is our most ancient and most worthy and, after all, our most pleasing responsibility. To cherish what remains of it, and to foster its renewal, is our only legitimate hope."[137]

I picture Wendell Berry curling his lip at the thought of a book about cities. Never a fan of density or frivolity, Berry would likely prepare one of his venomous diatribes, heaping scorn upon the very suggestion of cities as the intention of God.

So, the question now is, do we have to live in cities to be good? If God gave us a Garden but requires a City, does that mean we have to move downtown to be holy?

Of course not.

The City is a metaphor for cooperative work with God. A City is no more inherently spiritual than a rural community or an out-of-the-way farm. The point is not urbanity but cooperation. In the biblical sense, Berry's work on his farm is 'City-work' as much as that of a civil engineer.

This, I think, is what would frustrate Wendell Berry. He thinks of cities as parasites that only consume, only waste, and never produce. Similarly, theologian Jim Perkinson points out, "A city represents a masked structure of dependence on various 'elsewheres:' no city is able to grow its necessary foodstuffs and fabrics inside of its own borders or mine its needed metals and minerals from under its own feet. . . . A city, in this sense, is a large mouth, consuming an ever-growing torrent of resources and energies forcibly harvested from their points of 'natural' origin elsewhere."[138]

Berry and Perkinson are wrong to villainize cities. Cities are places of tremendous beauty and ingenuity, treating civilization to the application of skill and labor in architecture, economics, the arts, and culture. And the relationship of the City to the land, though more complex, is still much like that of the farm. Ecologists work in cities, and any protection the land receives comes from the centers of the population and not from those still living in the moss.

The City is a metaphor, but our cities are also pretty good examples for how we have to work together in order to survive. Some of us may prefer the country but the country, like the Garden, is just a way of talking about the things God gave us.

Biblically, cities are the result of cooperation with God. The opposite of a godly City is not a godly farm, but a godless City, a City left to ruin, a society turned into a cesspool. The thing that makes it perverse is not the "City" part but the "godless" part. The opposite of a godly Garden is not a skatepark, but an overgrown thicket populated by rats.

The virtue lies in cooperation. **The opposite of human cooperation can be both lack of cooperation and/or cooperation with an aberrant god.** Some cities, rather than giving themselves to God, have given themselves over to a false or foreign deity, whether something ancient like Ashtoreth or Baal, or something contemporary like Relevance or Fame.

Our efforts to cooperate with God matter regardless of the form they take. We can work with God as a hairdresser or a garbage collector, cooperating to heal the world as a doula or a dentist. **The specifics matter less than the intent, such that we all get to celebrate our work for God regardless of what that work might be.**

The land is the starting point. It was the original gift. But that gift came with instructions: fill the earth and subdue it.[139] There's some assembly required. At the end, God will want to know what we did with the gift. Did we watch it, or did we work it?[140]

How joyful are those who fear the LORD—
all who follow his ways!

You will enjoy the fruit of your labor. How joyful
and prosperous you will be!

Your wife will be like a fruitful grapevine, flourishing
within your home.

Your children will be like vigorous young olive trees
as they sit around your table.

That is the LORD's blessing for those who fear him.

May the LORD continually bless you from Zion.
May you see Jerusalem prosper as long as you live.

May you live to enjoy your grandchildren.
May Israel have peace!

◆

Psalm 128:1–6

IT ALL MATTERS

I have been a scuba diver for several years and have gone on hundreds of dives across North America. Three have been environmental rescue dives. I visited sites in crisis and worked with teams of volunteers to assist in ecological sustainability. I have no doubt God was pleased with my work in service to his Creation. Yet I am equally certain God is pleased by my work as an artist creating robot-themed lamps out of electrical conduits and junction boxes. I experience God's pleasure while creating weird housewares, just as I did while scraping mollusks and barnacles off underwater rock formations.

How can this be? **How can two totally different pursuits, one selfless and one frivolous, both serve as portals to God's pleasure?**

Simple. **There is no actual boundary between godly work and good work.** All work is good when we do it unto the Lord. The fact that we see ourselves in cooperation with God, regardless of what specifically we're doing, helps us understand that God's project of ongoing Creation is as varied as it is large.

The ideal human existence is not eternal leisure and endless vacation. Our fulfillment depends on creative, constructive work. **The work we do not only improves the world but us also.**

Our work is a significant part of our identity. And, again, I'm not referring to our jobs, but to our chosen and unique contributions to the world.

You might balk at this, thinking that you'd much prefer leisure to labor. Of course, for a time, we all would make that choice. (Golfers are especially prone to skipping work and may be the closest group of people on the planet for whom endless rounds of eighteen holes is preferable to just about any other activity.) But there inevitably comes a time when you want to do something. To make something. To fix something. To offer something to others. To contribute.

And so, we write. Or paint. Or build. Or solve. Or organize.

Even the most artistic pursuits are rightly considered work. Ask any writer if their prose falls off their pen absent effort. Ask any drummer if they've had to battle carpal tunnel syndrome or fix blisters while learning their rudiments. Ask any weekend gardener if the love they have for their backyard means they never experience muscle soreness, dehydration, or a stiff back.

Everything we do is work. And everything we do is worship. Or it can be. When we orient ourselves to our Creator, bringing our work to God as an offering.

Sometimes, when I go back and read this book, I'm tempted to replace the word *work* with *ministry* or *contribution* or *passion*. Even *play*. I like all these replacements and know they have some validity.

But then I remember that I never need encouragement to pursue my passions. I do however need a reminder that my work matters. All the hospital visits I've done, all the funerals, all the marriage counseling, all the teaching, all the experiments in homiletics and hermeneutics, liturgics, and missiology—it all matters. Even when some people are ungrateful. Even when some make derisive comments. Even when some wonder why I waste my time doing things of which they don't approve to benefit people they don't like to grow a church in which they have no investment.

It all matters.

Your work is the way you cooperate with God to heal the world. That's true whether you're a fireman or a salesclerk, a hobbyist or a scholar, a lineman or a piano teacher. What you do matters to God, it matters to us, and it matters to you. Your work shapes how you think of yourself. Your work gives you dignity and value in your own mind, demonstrating that you have the ability to shape and change the world. You have agency. You have power. You have responsibility. And you can experience great joy as you do all the Lord has placed within you to perform.

We are wired for this work. We want to work. We want to do good work. We want to do "work that matters for people who care."[142]

Even children work. We usually call it play, which is a healthy reminder that good work is enjoyable, voluntary, and imaginative. But playtime is often labor-intensive. Consider the child who spends days and days building a kingdom from wooden blocks. They're working. They get frustrated. They solve problems. They rarely take breaks. They're caught up in task-focused attention, enjoying the flow. Or consider the child who performs a puppet show or a solo dance recital. They make costumes. They design their stage and set. They position the audience. They create a beginning, middle, and end according to their vision for how the performance should unfold. That's work. It's good work because it's imaginative and voluntary and they exert control over their environment. But it's still work.

There are those who contend work is evil, a component of the Fall. They may suggest work is a corruption of Western society, a burden of the patriarchy, or a sinful and controlling mechanism of society meant to enslave.

They're right. The work they describe is all of those things.

But I'm not talking about the bone-crushing weariness associated with soulless labor. Not here. I'm talking about the work these same people undertake when they craft arguments and muse over biblical theology in order to make those statements. That didn't happen effortlessly. It was work to decry the condition of modern "work." God made us to work, but there will always be Pharaohs who force us to toil.

God says, "Eat freely."

Pharaoh says, "Make bricks."

God says, "Conserve and conceive."

Pharaoh says, "You shall not rest."

God says, "You shall have dominion."

Pharaoh says, "I will never let you go."

So, yes. There is toil that must be shrugged off, refused, and denied. There is work we should not do. There is work to which we must not succumb. We must always demand freedom from Pharaoh.

But once we're free, we're free to work.

And play and laugh and love and rejoice and sing and build and hope and dream.

The scripture uses the word *work* to describe all that. Agriculture and forestry and ecology are work, just as government and law enforcement are work. With every field we till or sculpture we craft, whether with plastics or pinewood or peach pits or paper, we move one step closer to the vision in Revelation of the City of God.

You must reclaim the dignity of what you do and what you have to offer. To be reminded that it all matters, and so do you.

Instead of saying, "I have to work," we can say, "I get to work."

You get to pour yourself into all that you do with all that you are. Some portion of that may be joyfully bagging groceries for strangers, just as some portion of that might be horticulture or poetry or film. Some portion of that might require you to offer unpleasant work to God and demonstrate the joy of the Spirit, just as some portion of that might be refusing to do work that robs you of your dignity. But you do not ever have to succumb to the drudgery and the banality of a life without passion or adventure or wonder or love. You have the choice to wake up and embrace life and your role in it.

God's City is beautifully adorned, wonderfully planned, symmetrically designed, and holistically organic. There's music and architecture, creativity and industry, community and laughter, good food and fine wine, with marvels and amazements upon which to gaze as we experience the unfettered presence of God. But those things all exist in the City of God because we made them alongside our Creator.

We have to make the world we want.

Let's get to work.

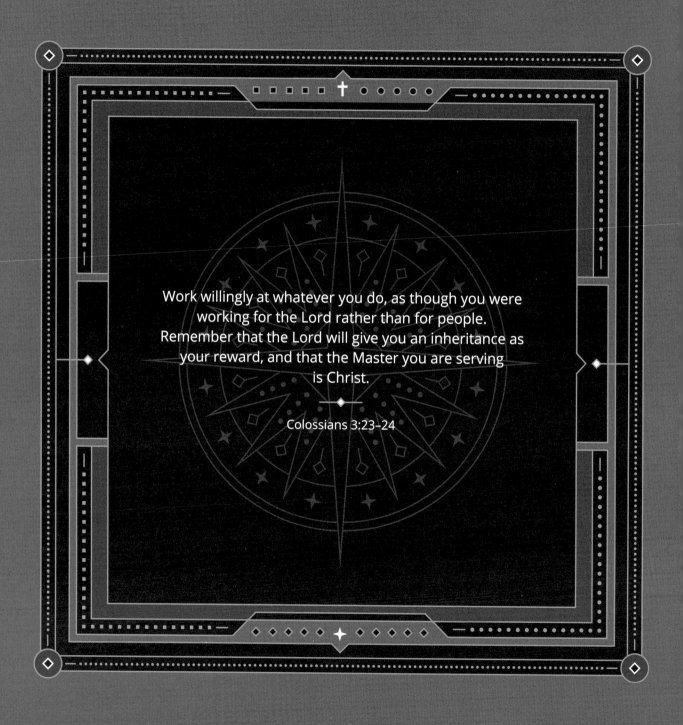

Work willingly at whatever you do, as though you were working for the Lord rather than for people. Remember that the Lord will give you an inheritance as your reward, and that the Master you are serving is Christ.

Colossians 3:23–24

THE CITY, THE KINGDOM,
AND HEAVEN

It takes a long time to grow a City. **It takes a long time to incubate a dream, especially the dream of the whole earth covered with God's glory.**[143] In the middle of our lives and the middle of our work we cannot lose sight of why we're doing the things we're doing. We're not simply working, but working as unto the Lord,[144] striving to ensure that all our efforts point toward the City "whose builder and maker is God."[145]

Three metaphors dominate biblical literature, each representing an aspect of God's people living in God's space according to God's way. These metaphors—the City, the Kingdom, and Heaven—work in harmony to help us envision a reality we can't quite see, understand, or comprehend alone.[146]

The City is about cooperation with God. Heaven is about the saturation of God's presence. The Kingdom is a metaphorical way of denoting our ruling activity with Christ, under Christ.

There is a place where God's presence and authority are obvious and dominant (Heaven).

Though we get partial access to that presence and authority as it breaks into our world (Kingdom), there will come a time when our cooperation with God as cocreators results in God's presence and authority being obvious and dominant everywhere (the City of God).

Heaven is the place where God's Kingdom has been fully manifested, and yet a time will come when that Heavenly Kingdom is fully manifested everyplace as the City of God.

George Eldon Ladd's classic theological work *The Gospel of the Kingdom*[147] introduces us to the concept that the Kingdom of God is already here but not yet fully realized. This already-not-yet distinction is critical for understanding how some things don't work the way we hoped, in the time we had, despite clear biblical indication that it should. Ladd uses plain language and common sense to talk about the fact that we are already living in God's kingdom on Earth as it is in Heaven,[148] but we don't yet fully experience all the benefits therein. **We live in a time between times, where God's rule and reign are breaking into this world with miraculous power and demonstrations of supernatural authority. Just not always.**

We're already living in God's Kingdom, but we're not yet full-time residents of Heaven. If the Kingdom was the only metaphor we had to understand about how God works and what God wants, we'd err on the side of spiritual lethargy. We'd pray, throwing our hands up in the air, resolving that if God wanted to do something, it would happen. Or not.

That's why God has given us the metaphor of the City, so we understand that **we are tasked to heal the world.** Thus, everything we do becomes holy. Our work is worship.[149] Our thoughts are prayer.[150] Our families are churches.[151] Our churches are conclaves of God's Kingdom.[152] Nothing we do can ever be reduced to mere activity. Everything we do is elevated in the presence of God.[153]

Every. Single. Thing.

From writing a letter to reading a book, from solving a puzzle to puzzling out a solution. **Everything we do works in two directions: as an action we take in space and time and as a manifestation of how we worship God, cultivating life on earth as it is in Heaven.**

In the Bible the word *Heaven* is a complicated term that refers to several things simultaneously. Heaven is the place where God is now, ruling and reigning over the cosmos.[154] Yet Heaven interpenetrates every place, such that God is everywhere even while technically still in Heaven.[155]

Heaven also refers to any place above the earth.[156] The skies are called the heavens. So are the stars. The sun and the moon are part of the heavens. This is why so many people perceive Heaven as being "up there." It's not, not any more than hell is down below, because Heaven isn't strictly a physical place. Heaven is also a way of being, a state in which things are the way God wants them to be. This is the Heaven with which you and I are most familiar. This is the version of Heaven we get to experience now, as a foretaste,[157] in anticipation of God's full and final cleanup of the world. Heaven is also the terminus point of all Creation.[158] Revelation concludes with a New Heaven, New Earth, and a New Jerusalem comprising a New Creation. These are all components of God's plan to make things right such that there is no longer any pain or hardship or evil or malcontent left anywhere. Heaven is also a metaphorical way of denoting God's ultimate locus of power and presence. **When we say we're "in Heaven" or that something is "heavenly," what we're really saying is that it feels good, like it should, and we're permitted to enjoy it, like we should.** To experience life on earth as it is in Heaven is to laugh without fear of mockery, to smile without bitter disappointment, to risk without fear of exposure, and to love without the worry of rejection.

We have been welcomed into God's Heavenly Kingdom,[159] adopted as heirs,[160] and given status as a royal priesthood.[161] We are permitted to enjoy good things in this life as signposts of God's blessing and a down payment toward God's future redemption of the world.[162]

Despite the fact that not everything will go well, nor will all things go well simultaneously, we are not forced to endure a life of unabashed misery until Christ returns. **We may not get to enjoy all of God's blessings now, but we definitely get to enjoy *some* of God's blessings now, as a down payment for a deluge of blessing later.**

We live in the time between times, where we work for the City of God amid the cities of men. We yearn for the final consummation of Heaven and earth in the New Creation, when God's Kingdom is fully manifest and the kingdom of our world becomes the Kingdom of our God,[163] when the City descends as Christ's Bride.[164] We serve our King in the ultimate Kingdom; but our knowledge of the City helps us to also understand that the King isn't looking for ladies-in-waiting but rather knights errant.

Because Christ doesn't intend to rule alone.[165]

This is a trustworthy saying:

If we die with him, we will also live with him.

If we endure hardship, we will reign with him.

If we deny him, he will deny us.

If we are unfaithful, he remains faithful, for he cannot deny who he is.

2 Timothy 2:11–13

28

NOT A PLACE BUT A PEOPLE

The New Jerusalem—the City of God—isn't a place, but a people.[166] We are the place where God's imagination, vocation, and connection are located.

Don't miss this. We are the City of God, and in God's promised future, the City is glorified and beautified so we become a perfect Bride for the Son of God.

"The most important city in the world," says theologian Jon Dennis, "is simply *God's people*. . . . They represent an enduring city, one that will outlast every other city . . . a city of light within a city of darkness."[167]

We are the center of God's government, God's creativity, and God's peace. Every place we are is the place where God is in control.[168] We are in God's roving Kingdom,[169] experiencing life on earth as it is in Heaven.[170]

This was difficult for me to accept because I don't often feel as though I'm experiencing all that the scripture promises. The idea that I'm the City of God seems insipid and vain. But then I realized I'm not the people of God. We are. It takes people, not just one person, coming together before God's City is manifest in the world.[171]

Consider the ecstasy of an especially intense prayer meeting. As a teenager I was full of zeal and passion for God. Together with my friends, we'd pray for hours, believing God would meet us and transform us. God did. God still does. Those meetings felt like sacred space, not because of the room they were in—they were in all sorts of rooms, but I can't recall what any of them looked like—but because, when we came together, we created a new kind of space entirely.

That's the City of God. That's the people of God gathering, binding, connecting, and believing. That's what happens when we come together—God is in our midst, bringing the world-changing power of mourning-to-mirth.

Martin Heidegger, the famous philosopher, said every person is actually a "*dasein*,"[172] which literally translates as "a being there." He meant that our existence happens in a particular time and place, and our identity cannot be separated from our location. Poet José Ortega y Gasset implied much the same, when he said, "Tell me the landscape in which you live, and I will tell you who you are."[173]

All experience is placed experience because the things that happen to us happen some-where. The uniqueness of being God's City is that this City is a place we create. Anywhere, at any time we come together. The City of God is a place we inhabit, just as it is a place we manifest. It's the place where we live together in the presence of the Lord.

Our responsibility then is to create that space more often, to recognize the power of that space, and to enter into it as frequently as possible. It's not as simple as getting Christians together for coffee. It requires us to acknowledge the Spirit and make ourselves available to

God and to one another. That *could* happen over coffee, but it rarely happens without our intention to foster it or our desire to experience it.

I hope you have that desire in all you do and that you cultivate that desire in anticipation of all God promises you will enjoy in eternity.

You are coming to Christ, who is the living cornerstone of God's temple. He was rejected by people, but he was chosen by God for great honor.

And you are living stones that God is building into his spiritual temple. What's more, you are his holy priests. Through the mediation of Jesus Christ, you offer spiritual sacrifices that please God.

1 Peter 2:4–5

AN INVISIBLE WAR

Our world is sick. That world sickness has festered, creating societal sores—a spiritual cancer that eats away at the people we know and love as surely as its physical counterpart. And in this civilization of deterioration, we are called to be fathers and mothers, sons and daughters, parents and protectors.

How?

How can we contend against powers we cannot see, measure, or predict? How are we to enthrone Christ in our homes? How are we to dethrone the competing powers of this world in our hearts?

Perhaps the simplest, oldest answer is also the best.

A weary traveler, after months of journeying, stopped at the hut of an old man. The old man gave him water and food, as he did to all who passed by. The old man knew it was more than a thousand miles to the traveler's destination, and so he told his guest. The traveler looked down the dusty road as it fumbled off into the distance, discouraged, and asked, "How can I make it a thousand miles?" to which the old man replied, "A step at a time."

How do we make Christ Lord of our hearts, Lord of our homes, Lord of our world? A step at a time.

When we were ejected from Eden, God's plan for Eden to expand in ever-increasing development became compromised. Those who remained faithful to God continued to cooperate, and the scriptures refer to them and to their work as the City of God.[174] But there were others who sought to employ God's gameplan without God, hoping to counterfeit God's promised blessings. Their work has been labeled the City of Man, and it relies upon exploitation and injustice.

The good news is that every time we cooperate with the Lord, we strengthen the City of God.[175] The People of God are the City within all cities working to heal the world. We live according to different values.[176] We observe different practices.[177] In our homes, children are held in high esteem,[178] the blessed poor are given a place of honor,[179] service is valued over power,[180] enemies are redeemed as friends,[181] life is filled with faith and free from worry,[182] and those who mistreat us are held up in prayer to God.[183]

Our invisible war will not be over soon, but that doesn't mean we won't win the battle for our children, for our churches, and for our minds and hearts and souls. We fight for the day when our great joys will never diminish, when our smiles will never fade, when our celebrations will never tire.[184] We work toward that future reality when the kingdom of this world becomes the kingdom of our God.[185]

It is coming soon,[186] and we will welcome Christ as it does.

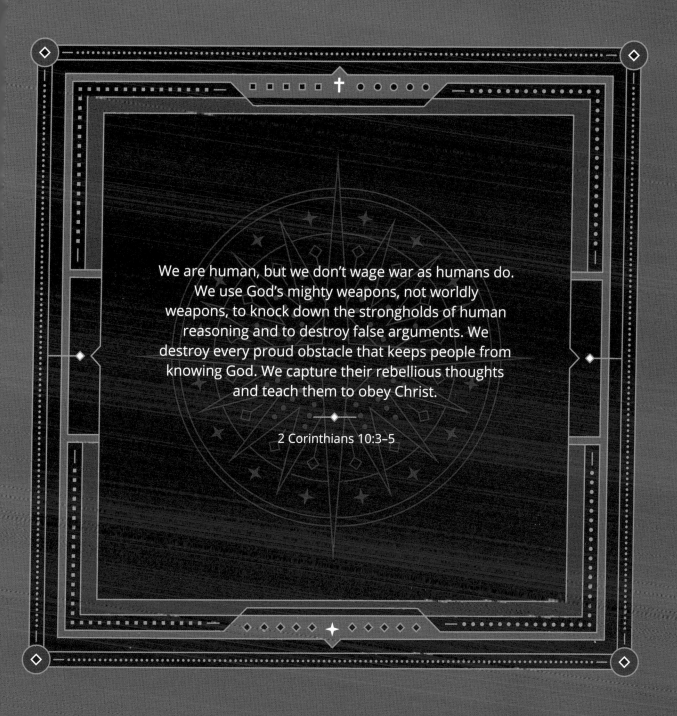

We are human, but we don't wage war as humans do. We use God's mighty weapons, not worldly weapons, to knock down the strongholds of human reasoning and to destroy false arguments. We destroy every proud obstacle that keeps people from knowing God. We capture their rebellious thoughts and teach them to obey Christ.

2 Corinthians 10:3–5

NOT CULTURE BUT CHRIST

How do we live in the world without being contaminated by it? How can we live as the "light of the world" and the "City on a hill?"

Sometimes people think God wants us to create an entirely separate Christian world inside this one, to retreat from our culture. They believe we should live in Christian cities with Christian governments, following Christian laws about Christian morality. But this doesn't make any sense. How can we introduce the world to Christ if we're never involved with it?

Others suggest we're supposed to transform our world, replacing worldly things with Christian things, or to take it a step further, to turn worldly things into Christian things. Here we'd listen to Christian music and watch Christian films while wearing Christian clothing and eating Christian food. But, again, this seems strange. It puts all the emphasis on *things*, as though our commission to enter the world is simply so we can flaunt our plunder.

Of course, we're not the first people to be asking these questions; nor are we the first people to propose these solutions. The Epistle to Diognetus is one of my favorite ancient documents. We don't know much about it, only that it serves as one of the earliest defenses of Christian character. The author had watched Christians for some time and wrote this letter to commend them to his friend.

Whenever I am confronted by the questions I posed earlier, I think back on this letter. It's great evidence that Christians actually did what Christ commanded us to do, that at least some of our predecessors got it right, and that their faithful witness was effective. **They didn't focus on culture but on Christ. They weren't consumed with fixing everything, only with allowing Christ to fix them.**

Here's the best excerpt:

> Christians are not distinguished from the rest of humanity by country, language, or custom. For nowhere do they live in cities of their own, nor do they speak some unusual dialect, nor do they practice an eccentric lifestyle. . . . While they live in both Greek and barbarian cities, as each one's lot was cast, and follow the local customs in dress and food and other aspects of life, at the same time they demonstrate the remarkable and admittedly unusual character of their own citizenship. They live in their own countries, but only as aliens; they participate in everything as citizens, and endure everything as foreigners. Every foreign country is their fatherland, and every fatherland is foreign. They marry like everyone else, and have children, but they do not expose their offspring. They share their food but not their wives. They are "in the flesh," but do not live "according to the flesh." They live on earth, but their citizenship is in heaven. They obey the established laws; indeed in their private lives they transcend the laws. They love everyone, and by everyone they are persecuted. They are unknown, yet they are condemned; they are put to death, yet they are brought to life. They are poor, yet they make many rich; they are in need of everything, yet they abound in everything. They are dishonored, yet they are glorified in their dishonor;

they are slandered, yet they are vindicated. They are cursed, yet they bless; they are insulted, yet they offer respect. When they do good, they are punished as evildoers; when they are punished, they rejoice as though brought to life. . . . Those who hate them are unable to give a reason for their hostility.[187]

Toward the end of his letter, Diognetus's friend remarks, "In a word, **what the soul is in a body, the Christians are in the world.**"[188]

That's our calling, our high and holy identity: to live as Christ, to function as a kind of sacred germ within society. We show others what it means to love without possessiveness or selfish motivation or desire to control. We have been called to remove the taint from finance, learning to live with little instead of lusting for more. We are here to regenerate health and well-being, kindness and concern, joy, peace, faith, hope, and love.

We are the antibodies to the sickness of our world.

We are the City of God among the cities of men.

Build homes, and plan to stay. Plant gardens, and eat the food they produce. Marry and have children. Then find spouses for them so that you may have many grandchildren. Multiply! Do not dwindle away! And work for the peace and prosperity of the city where I sent you into exile. Pray to the LORD for it, for its welfare will determine your welfare.

Jeremiah 29:5–7

A NEW LANGUAGE

† During the earliest season of Christianity after Christ, whenever someone came to faith, they were accompanied by their household. If a woman became a follower of Jesus, it wasn't long before her husband, children, friends, and neighbors became Christ-followers too. Sometimes that conversion by association occurred because of the simple magnetism of the gospel story—it is, after all, amazing—but always that conversion by association was facilitated by the intentional efforts of Christ-followers to introduce their friends and family to God.

From those original households, the church began to grow. Not only did the number of congregations grow, but the congregations themselves experienced growth. Which means those original households expanded.

We want to follow suit, but we're afraid

The chief obstacle to our growth is fear. We're afraid that, once we start spouting our religion, people will either grow shy or hostile. Either they won't want to be our friends, or they'll decide they want to be our adversaries.

I think this is why John relays the scene of the two witnesses in Revelation 11 who first proclaim the gospel and are then martyred for their testimony. They serve as both an example and a warning: faithful witness results in persecution.

It will cost us something to follow Jesus, and it will cost us even more to invite others to do the same. In fact, whenever Paul speaks of being a sacrifice, "without exception he is referring to his ministry of furthering his witness to unbelieving Gentiles."[189]

Evangelism is the context in which Paul proclaimed Christians are a "sweet perfume . . . by those who are being saved."[190] That aroma is the fragrance of temple sacrifice, a useful reminder that "the blood of the martyrs is the seed of the church."[191] Also included in Paul's definition of sacrifice are sacrificial giving[192] and investment in other people's spiritual development,[193] even going so far as to claim he was being "pouring it out like a liquid offering to God, just like your faithful service is an offering to God."[194]

The purpose of our cooperation with God is to ensure that God's government, God's creativity, and God's peace cover the earth, that the people who were once not a people become the people of God.[195]

The only way that's going to happen is if we take our commission seriously.

Fulfilling this commission isn't just a matter of bullheaded determination. **We need to not only enter the culture but challenge it and also appeal to those within it.** Paul never wholly criticized nor totally affirmed any culture, but instead showed them that the means through which they pursued good things ultimately became self-defeating.[196]

Critically engaging culture allowed Paul to preach to conservative religious people,[197] peasant polytheists,[198] sophisticated pagans,[199] Christian elders,[200] a hostile Jewish mob,[201] and elite government officials from both Rome and Israel.[202] But it's also the same strategy that

will allow us to witness to conservative employers, peasant neighbors, sophisticated colleagues, Christian friends, hostile adherents to other faiths, and elite government officials in our own city.

In order for our strategy to be effective, we will need to contextualize our message. This means telling people good news in a way they understand, find persuasive, and must ultimately decide to reject or accept. It means finding ways to write on the whiteboard until our friends, neighbors, families, and peers finally begin to grasp the power of God's story. That doesn't mean they will always like God's story, or even find it compelling, but they have to—at the very least—understand it.

When the books of the Second Testament were finally translated into *Koine* Greek, the gospel spread like wildfire. *Koine* was the common tongue of the Roman Empire, and once people could access the gospel story in a way they could understand it, the gospel took hold of their imagination, their passion, and ultimately their allegiance.

That's what we're always looking for: a new *Koine*.

We need to be increasingly bold about our faith in Christ. We need to expand the sphere of our influence, love, and hospitality. We need to be intentional about sharing with our family and friends, and we should be intentional about growing the number of friends, neighbors, coworkers, and peers we invite to become a part of our lives.

It's not rocket science, but it is effective: we expand the sphere of our love, influence, and hospitality by first getting involved in the world around us, challenging the corrupt influences in that world, and then showing the people around us a better way.

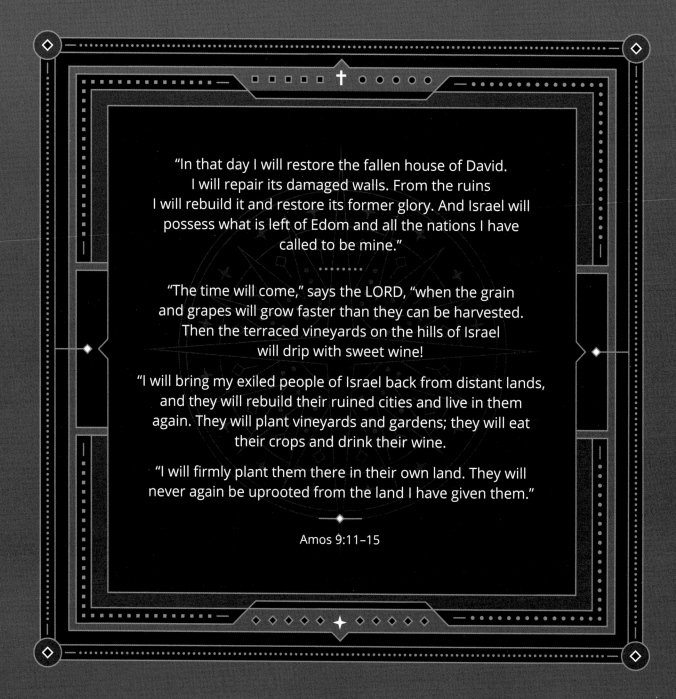

"In that day I will restore the fallen house of David.
I will repair its damaged walls. From the ruins
I will rebuild it and restore its former glory. And Israel will
possess what is left of Edom and all the nations I have
called to be mine."

"The time will come," says the LORD, "when the grain
and grapes will grow faster than they can be harvested.
Then the terraced vineyards on the hills of Israel
will drip with sweet wine!

"I will bring my exiled people of Israel back from distant lands,
and they will rebuild their ruined cities and live in them
again. They will plant vineyards and gardens; they will eat
their crops and drink their wine.

"I will firmly plant them there in their own land. They will
never again be uprooted from the land I have given them."

Amos 9:11–15

YOU CANNOT SEPARATE CHRIST
FROM THE CHURCH

⚸ **We can't separate Christ from his church.** Or vice versa. If he's the head and we're the body,[203] it's hard to conceive of a scenario, in which either survives without remaining connected. And all that jazz about "being a Christian but not being part of a church" is really just semantics. If you're a Christian you're part of the Church whether you wish it or not. If you're a churchless Christian, that simply means your local congregation has an average attendance of one and suffers the same problems as the rest of the world's congregations—people aren't generous, nobody volunteers, few are willing to put others' needs before their own, there's little in the way of structured discipleship, and so on. The only difference is that, in the one-man congregation, you aren't allowed to blame anybody else for its deficiencies.

Our churches are inextricably linked to the multimillennial community of God's people, comprised of a Great Cloud of Witnesses.[204] Some churches are better than others—more intentional, more meaningful, more interesting, more accurate—but every church that serves Christ is part of his body.[205]

Sadly, there are times when the Church tries to do God's things without God. It seems foolish, and it is, but we all know mission drift is a critical concern. More and more, churches deprioritize Christ and focus instead on any number of distracting topics—politics, justice, innovation, technology, charity, education. Obviously, these are important issues, but—and here's where we feel nervous—many of our friends have fallen away from Jesus because of how much they've fallen in with something Jesus provides. They've abandoned their first love.[206] No longer are they interested in Christ, but in Christian politics; no longer are they following the Spirit, now they're focused on spiritual justice; no longer are they following the Way, they just want to point out how other Christians have missed the point.

We're losing the Giver for the gift.

We have become consumed with getting whatever we think Jesus ought to supply. But, as Stephen King warned in his magnum opus, *The Dark Tower*, "Greed in a good cause is still greed."

When this happens—when the people of God decide they would rather be just the people—we begin to function like the cities of Cain, and destruction inevitably ensues.

> How ridiculous, how grotesque is bravado of naked little man. . . . Man shouts, "I will stop the whole mess, I will put it in order." . . .

> Poor little man. You failed to notice that you are not dealing with flesh and blood, but with Thrones, and Powers, and Dominations which are attacking you, grinding you under, dominating you from every side, and that the Devil's last trick is to make you think that you can put order back into this chaos, that you are going to get spiritually big enough to control the world! To be sure, the Devil will offer you this spiritual growth. He offered the very same thing, with the same goal in mind, to Jesus Christ. But with him the offer failed.[207]

We must keep our focus on Jesus Christ. We live in the company of priests and kings.[208] We're faithful witnesses to the God of the living, who calls things that are not as though they are[209] and who makes all things new.[210] Justice will come, but Jesus will bring it.[211] Peace will reign, but it emanates from the sacred heart of Christ.[212] The poor will be made rich and the lame will leap for joy,[213] but their transformation will come through one Lord, one God, one faith, and one baptism.[214] Apart from him, we can do nothing.[215]

Christ is the visible image of the invisible God.
He existed before anything was created and is
supreme over all creation, for through him God created
everything in the heavenly realms and on earth.
He made the things we can see and the things we can't
see—such as thrones, kingdoms, rulers, and
authorities in the unseen world. Everything was created
through him and for him. He existed before anything
else, and he holds all creation together.

Christ is also the head of the church, which is his body.
He is the beginning, supreme over all who rise
from the dead. So he is first in everything. For God in all
his fullness was pleased to live in Christ, and through
him God reconciled everything to himself. He made peace
with everything in heaven and on earth by means of
Christ's blood on the cross.

Colossians 1:15–20

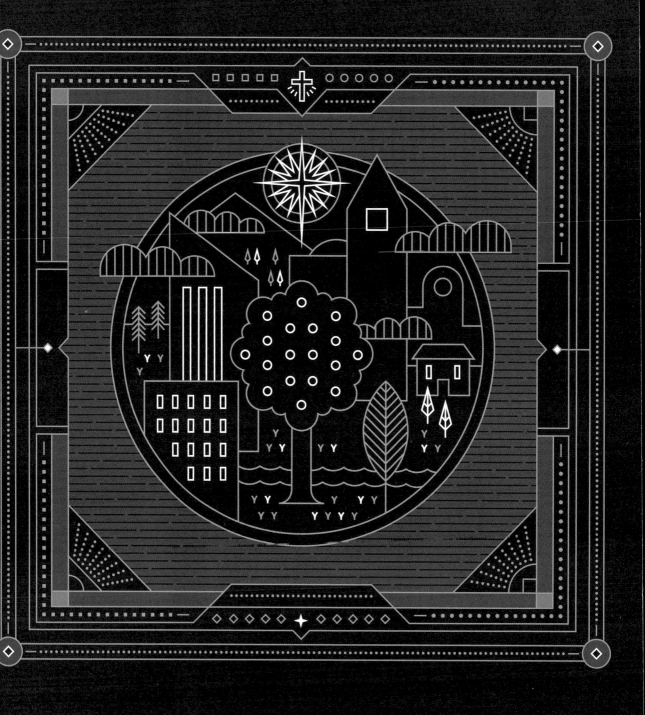

In this final section of the book, we turn our attention to the ways in which we personally and practically demonstrate our commitment to the Edenic mandate. Knowing our work in this world is not merely about achievement, creativity, ingenuity, or dreams, what else is involved in our commitment to God and the final plan to heal the world?

In the famous question of theologian Francis Schaeffer, "How shall we then live?"

RESIDENT ALIENS

Zygmunt Bauman is one of the greatest sociologists of the twentieth century. He understands community, society, and human relationships like few others.[216] One of his favorite means of talking about the ways we interact is to distinguish between "tourists" and "vagabonds." I've always felt this distinction needs to be further developed to include "vagrants" and "resident aliens" in order to better understand God's calling for people to be a City of Light within the cities of darkness.

A vagrant is a hostile person living downtown. Vagrants are often listless and purposeless, but if provoked will quickly turn violent. **Many Christians live as vagrants.** They have no noble purpose but seem to be everywhere, drawing attention to themselves. If approached, Christians can lash out and do great harm to those around them yet never seem willing to accept responsibility for their actions. Some Christians seem convinced violence is necessary.

Vagabonds, by contrast, sleep on park benches and keep their libations in brown paper sacks. They are rootless and without family. **Christians can also be vagabonds**, pitiful creatures, always trying to solicit sympathy for their suffering. They wonder why the world doesn't help them, growing frustrated and despondent that their plight isn't addressed.

Tourists are people who visit downtown but take no responsibility for the City. They look and laugh, spend a little money and go shopping, but the only legacy they leave behind is their spare change. **Some Christians play tourist.** They taste Christianity's goods and enjoy their stay but never leave their mark. They're players, not producers.

It's clear God never intended us to be tourists, vagabonds, or vagrants. We are citizens of Heaven, but we live on earth.[217] We are not native to our earthly City, and it has been so long since we lived "at home" that we hardly feel like immigrants either.

The best way to describe us is as resident aliens. **We're from *there*, but we live *here*.** We still do heavenly things quite naturally, but we also commit ourselves to the good of the earth; we live by earthly rules, we obey earthly government, and we participate in earthly community.[218]

We're musicians and artists and workers and daughters—sure—but first, we are the people of God. We are creators created by the Creator to perpetuate Creation. We are people marked by God's government, God's creativity, and God's peace.

We need to remind one another of our Garden origins and our Garden-City calling; we need clusters of believers who refuse to give up on God's dream to heal the world; we need extended, adoptive families of men and women who act as surrogate moms and dads to those without healthy role models; we need people who will devote their lives to Christ, not just their weekends.

We have such a place. It's the Church.

Every time the Church reminds the world that God is at work, "God gets a foothold in man's world."[219]

God keeps working with and through the Church. God is helping people learn to forgive and reminding us we can't just sit around and expect things to sort themselves out on their own. God wants us to get back on our feet. God will help, but not if we're just going to watch. Some people think nothing will ever be good again. They're wrong. Others think the real answer to all our problems is to fix the government. Still others think technology will sort everything out.

They're wrong, too.[220]

The only way things are going to get any better—for you, for me, and for everybody else stuck halfway in-between—is if we remember God has called us to rise above our circumstances. **We have to work even when we don't feel like it. We have to try even when we feel discouraged. We have to believe even when we're full of doubt. We have to give even when we feel poor. We have to love even when we feel hurt. We have to trust even when we feel betrayed.**

Christianity can deteriorate into religion instead of living up to the calling of our founder. Yet everything Christ did was to get us back on track with what God did in the beginning. That's why Paul says Jesus Christ recapitulated us,[221] a word which means he undid and redid all our wrongs into rights. Christ became the Second Adam,[222] demonstrating the continuity between our New Creation as Christians and our original Creation as human beings.[223]

In the Garden of Eden, God gave us a gameplan for how to live in blessing. We were meant to create alongside our Creator, to draw together the resources of Creation, to bring wise order to the Garden, and to release human potential. But we got off track. We usually do.

The good news is that God has a way of setting us straight, sometimes even before we realize it.

Just when we think God is out of tricks, another hand comes into play. To paraphrase one of my favorite theologians, Jaques Ellul, God always shows up in our God-proofed rooms.[224] And when God arrives, it's always to remind us of who we were meant to become:

Creators cooperating with our Creator in the ongoing work of Creation.

Resident Aliens.

A Royal Priesthood. A Holy Nation.

The City of God amid the cities of men.

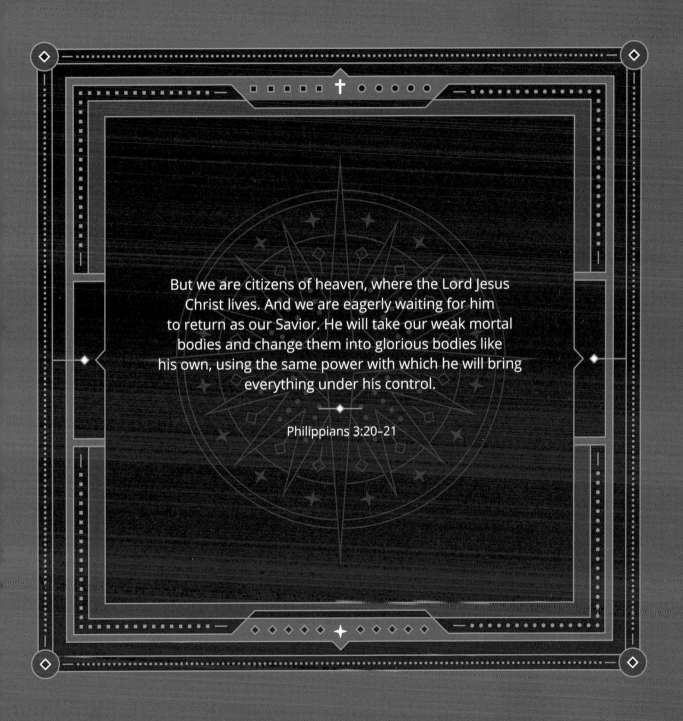

But we are citizens of heaven, where the Lord Jesus Christ lives. And we are eagerly waiting for him to return as our Savior. He will take our weak mortal bodies and change them into glorious bodies like his own, using the same power with which he will bring everything under his control.

Philippians 3:20–21

GIVE!

We are God's emissaries to the world around us. We are the "aroma of Christ,"[225] his "witnesses,"[226] and his "light."[227] As such, our energy for living well proceeds from the fathomless reservoir of God's Spirit. We know what it means to "silence the ignorant talk of foolish people" by doing good[228] and counter accusations that we warrant prosecution.[229] We repay evil with blessing and insult with gentleness.[230] And we're not finished. We must do more, be more, give more of ourselves, give more of our time, give more of our attention, until there is nothing left to give because there is nothing left to do, because God is "all in all."[231]

One of the defining characteristics of the first Christians was their care for the poor, both inside and outside their community. In a world of darkness, those who offer help are like shining lights.

Jesus assumes his followers will be givers in every way and on every occasion. God has blessed us so we can be a blessing to others, and the flow of blessing is not aimless. "God's gifts flow to us so they can flow through us."[232] God wants to create givers who give in divine emulation. All of this leads me to believe we should not need charity but be among those able to supply it.

I know it's tricky to talk about money, but the greatest spiritual adversary in contemporary Western society—and there's lots of competition—is Mammon.

Mammon was the name of an ancient deity representing all worldly goods. Sometimes we translate Mammon as "money," but Mammon was bigger than that, and more comprehensive.

Roman homes often had shrines to gods. Idols lived in these shrines, stone statues that decorated the shelves and before whom the homeowners would burn incense and pray. Mammon was a common idol in such a home, but Jesus warned that Mammon wasn't just a knickknack. Mammon is a spiritual power, and the more time and attention we give to Mammon, the more dangerous it becomes.

One of Jesus' most famous sayings is, "You cannot serve both God and Mammon."[233]

There is a spiritual contest at work in our cities, pitting the Spirit of God against the selfishness of humanity. Nowhere is this battle more apparent than in how we employ our possessions.

Jesus warned that we might become possessed by our possessions.

The best way to de-power Mammon is by being generous. And the truth is that there are few joys in life that compare with giving.

I learned from a good friend that **wealth can be an icon pointing people toward their Creator.** At the time, I didn't know my friend had considerable wealth. He didn't flaunt it. He didn't live in an exceptional house. He loved his family, served his church, and possessed

admirable Christian character. When I realized he was rich I became angry, as though I had been betrayed. But my friend kept pushing me about wealth, asking me questions I didn't have good answers for.

Questions like: Is giving an obligation or a privilege? Are we ever allowed to enjoy anything? Is work godly? If we work, should we not be compensated fairly? What composes faithful stewardship? Who is responsible for providing for my family? What legacy will I leave behind so that others will know I devoted my life to God? What kind of father does God want me to be, and how will I best be able to imitate God through generosity to my children?

I realized I only knew two answers about money: first, you should give it all away; and second, God loves the poor.

Of course God loves the poor—God loves the whole world, so there's no scenario in which the poor are rightfully excluded. But God doesn't only love the poor, and God doesn't require we destitute ourselves, demanding others assume our expenses since we can no longer look after ourselves. That would be asinine, since people who cannot take care of their families are roundly criticized in the New Testament.[234]

My friend had been using his resources faithfully to help others, to bless others, and to prepare for a future in which others would benefit from his hard work and know God. He did things in our community, demonstrating to the world—not just to the church, but equally to people who were still deciding if God was worth knowing—that he was committed to the common good.

Once I realized wealth could be an icon, I realized anything could point people to God: success, fame, even power, even sex. The only determining factor is us; what we do and what we say about what we have.

Our world is full of false gods and fraudulent idols, full of people and things and occurrences that focus attention on themselves, that demand they be worshipped instead of God. But most things are spiritually neutral. The only determining factor is us. Will we live with a priestly orientation, turning everything around us into an icon? Or will we continue to let things be what they are, content to stand off to one side as frustrated critics?

We have to realize that frustration and critique are idols of another kind, and that our posture of impatience toward privilege distracts us from seeing the privileged as people. We have to pray for God to soften our hearts, so we don't make idols out of iconoclasts.

Grace is free. Love abounds. The Kingdom is breaking into our world through our cooperative efforts as the City of God within the cities of men. Enjoy what you have,[235] and stay busy with all that you love,[236] but remember that you have been given much so you can be generous often.[237] This pleases God,[238] and for such largesse you will be rewarded.[239]

And what is your reward?

Joy.

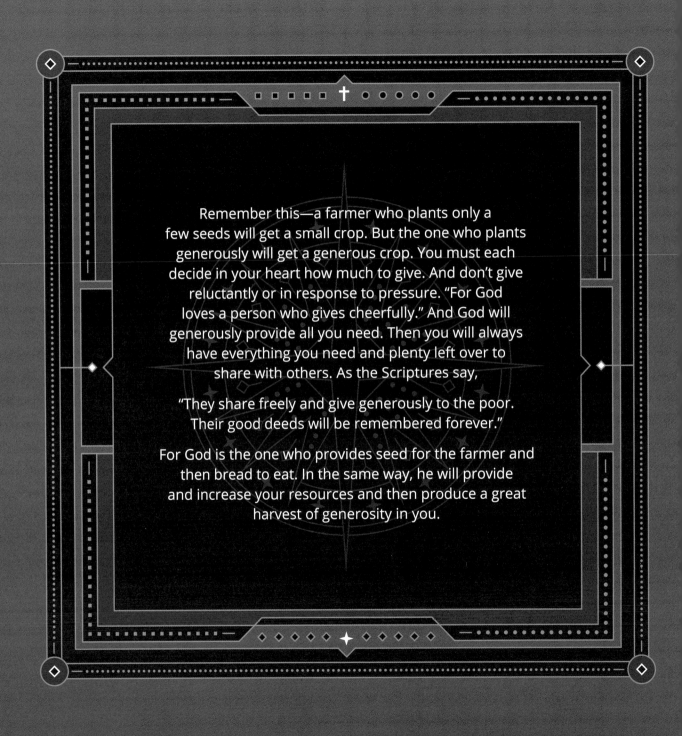

Remember this—a farmer who plants only a
few seeds will get a small crop. But the one who plants
generously will get a generous crop. You must each
decide in your heart how much to give. And don't give
reluctantly or in response to pressure. "For God
loves a person who gives cheerfully." And God will
generously provide all you need. Then you will always
have everything you need and plenty left over to
share with others. As the Scriptures say,

"They share freely and give generously to the poor.
Their good deeds will be remembered forever."

For God is the one who provides seed for the farmer and
then bread to eat. In the same way, he will provide
and increase your resources and then produce a great
harvest of generosity in you.

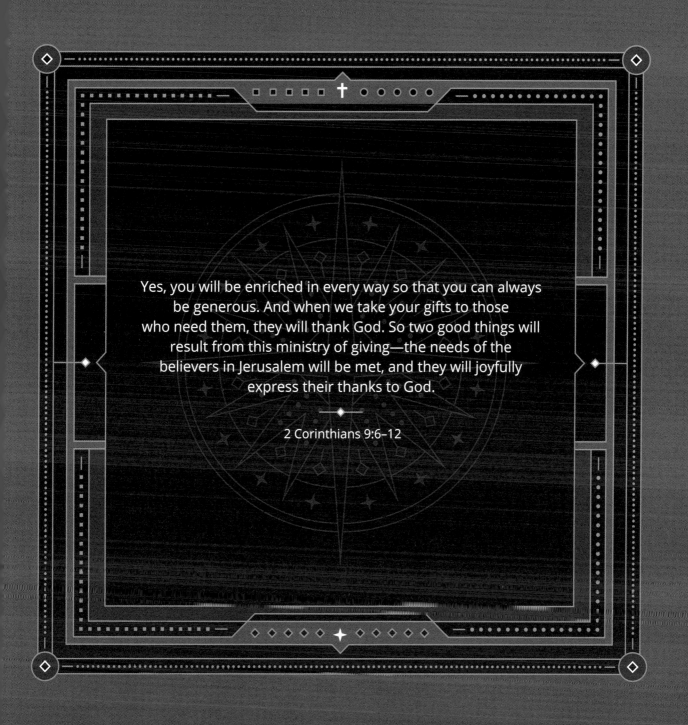

Yes, you will be enriched in every way so that you can always be generous. And when we take your gifts to those who need them, they will thank God. So two good things will result from this ministry of giving—the needs of the believers in Jerusalem will be met, and they will joyfully express their thanks to God.

2 Corinthians 9:6–12

HOUSE CHURCH

Four different times in Paul's letters, "specific congregations are designated by the phrase *hē kat' oikon* (+ possessive pronoun) *ekklēsia*, which may tentatively translate 'the assembly at N's household.'"[240] This terminology didn't just refer to the location of the church meeting, but to the basic unit of society from which the congregation arose.

The church in the Second Testament spread quickly from *oikos* to *oikos*—from house to house, virally. *Oikos* best translates as "family," though it means "household." The concept of the household was much more elastic then than now. Household (and "family") was not limited to blood relatives, but also included friends, coworkers, slaves, servants, employees, and neighbors. Anyone under your protection was in your household.

In today's parlance, **your household would be comprised of your "people."** It's everyone who would come to your graduation party, everyone whom you'd want to come to your birthday or wedding or retirement party.

There are radical implications hidden in a simple statement like "as for me and my family, we will serve the LORD."[241] When a person decided their entire household was making a decision for Christ, they then accepted the responsibility of making that decision stick.

In the case of the Philippian jailer,[242] that meant he would have had to go home and explain to his wife, his children, and all his friends and family that there was a man named Jesus who claimed to be God incarnate,

> . . . that he was crucified, he rose from the dead,
> . . . he promised his followers they would also rise from the dead,
> . . . he sent his Spirit to live in those followers now in anticipation of literal new life later on,
> . . . those followers gathered regularly to learn and give money and participate in charitable activity,
> . . . but they were persecuted for their religion,
> . . . this persecution was worth it,
> . . . and the jailer's entire household would now be expected to share in that persecution because they would begin following Jesus also.

Can you fathom having that conversation with your spouse, let alone everyone you consider part of your social circle? I can't get my wife to buy the kind of coffee I like unless I go with her to the grocery store; how could I ever convince her of the resurrection of a God in whom she didn't believe?

No matter how difficult it was, the earliest Christians accepted the responsibility of introducing their families to Christ. They loved their families so much they were willing to risk awkward conversations, potential arguments, heated discussions, and short-term fallout in order to secure their immortal souls.

How can we do anything less?

How can we stand in the long line of Christian people who, for thousands of years, have been enduring remarkable hardship, tribulation, and suffering without being ashamed of our unwillingness to raise our families as people who belong to the Lord?

These household churches started out independent from one another, but soon they began to network. Each *oikos* was like a node in a complex system spreading rapidly through the Roman Empire, until the connections became so strong that when you visited another *oikos* it felt like you were still at home. There were differences here and there, of course, but they all had the same DNA: Jesus is Lord.

If you picture the known world in the first century as a massive City, then you must also picture it as a city of darkness. The people of God became the light of the world,[243] and as they began to connect to one another, the light became a kind of City schematic all on its own. **The church became the City of Light within the city of darkness.** That's the way it's supposed to be. That's the way it still is.

We're not just "being good." Not just "leading our families." Our efforts, however mundane moment to moment, are nevertheless part of God's plans to heal the world.

Every effort you make to restrain your anger, to act upon wisdom instead of upon mood, to think critically instead of temperamentally, to overlook an offense instead of taking the bait, to assist those in need instead of turning a blind eye, to manifest creativity and intelligence and industry instead of lethargy and disregard, to be active instead of remaining passive . . . every effort counts toward God's plans to heal the world in you, through you, and with you.

When we become part of the Church, we establish patterns of hope and love for the people around us. Our coworkers, our children, our friends, and our neighbors all see the efforts we make to live distinct from the fragmented and cynical world. They recognize that you're part

of another way of being, of living, of enjoyment, of happiness, and of hopefulness. You are the City within the city. You are among the people of God, and your behaviors and your spirit are normalizing and sacralizing Abundant Life for all who care to observe.

Never forget this.

And don't you dare let your family forget it either.

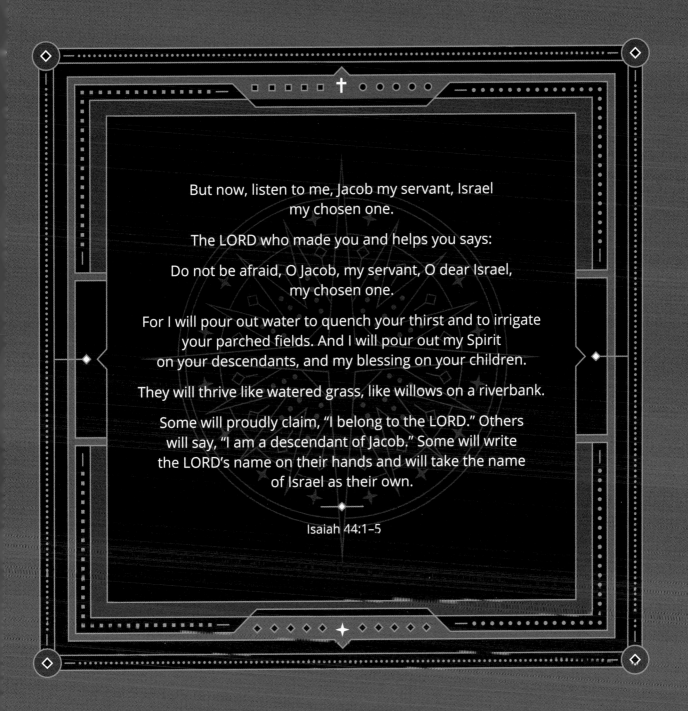

But now, listen to me, Jacob my servant, Israel
my chosen one.

The LORD who made you and helps you says:

Do not be afraid, O Jacob, my servant, O dear Israel,
my chosen one.

For I will pour out water to quench your thirst and to irrigate
your parched fields. And I will pour out my Spirit
on your descendants, and my blessing on your children.

They will thrive like watered grass, like willows on a riverbank.

Some will proudly claim, "I belong to the LORD." Others
will say, "I am a descendant of Jacob." Some will write
the LORD's name on their hands and will take the name
of Israel as their own.

Isaiah 44:1–5

CHRIST REFUELS

It would be a mistake to believe that all we need to do is try harder, work longer, or do more in order to please God. I realize that's an inherent danger in a book like this—that you might feel compelled to strive when what I'm trying to advocate is that you would experience abundant life, recognizing that all your efforts are offerings unto the Lord.

But you are not an inexhaustible resource. Once you start spending yourself, you stop being the person God has called you to be.

This happens to all of us. We become irritable with the people we love, stingy with our money, jealous of our time, defensive about our character, dismissive about our faith, and harsh in our estimation of other peoples' suffering.

The problem is that our greatest resource is also our greatest treasure. The biggest bargaining chip we have is also the thing we ought to protect above everything else. The one thing we're tempted to give away is just about the only thing we should never surrender: ourselves.

Something happens to us when we have to keep fighting all the time. **We grow tired. We become restless and dis-eased.** By *dis-eased* I mean the things that ought to be easy are difficult and unenjoyable.

Life feels more complicated, frustrating, and tiresome than it should. It's not because things are tough but because we the fear they will always be this tough. Or worse.

But there's good news! Regardless of how difficult our circumstances are, God promises to elevate us and sustain us.[244] The Lord promises life, strength, and hope for all who draw upon the Spirit.[245] "Salvation comes from our God,"[246] for "everyone who calls on the name of the LORD will be saved."[247]

Once, when I was at my lowest, and I wasn't sure God was listening—when I felt hopeless and afraid, thinking my life was over and I had nowhere to go—I prayed. Don't get me wrong, I pray often, but that's my point. There was nothing special about this prayer. I just prayed. I wasn't articulate. I wasn't fancy. I'm not sure what I said. But as I was praying, someone came to me and placed a hand upon my shoulder. That person prayed with me, which allowed me to stop praying and just rest. I was afraid I would fall asleep during the prayer, but I wept instead. And the Lord gave me something I hadn't realized I'd lost: God gave me the confidence that I had been seen and that I was not alone.

You are not alone.

Our world works contrary to God's design, and much of our struggle results from this conflict. We were made for God's world, but we're stuck in this one. The scripture says we're part of the City of God amid the cities of men, and that bilocational dissonance makes every good thing more elusive than it ought to be.

Good news—God has lots of strength to loan, and God will not charge interest.

Everything in this world seeks to commodify us, to turn our lives into something that can be traded, bought, used up, and ultimately thrown away. God is the only exception. God may require that we deplete ourselves,[248] but only so we can be filled again.[249] Whereas other things will use us, God promises to renew us day by day.[250]

I have been burned out at work, burned out on relationships, and burned out on hobbies as diverse as travel, exercise, and the arts. The only way I ever get unburned is through Christ. He is the Healer, Sustainer, Restorer, Redeemer, and Creator.[251]

As we dream about our lives, may we not neglect God. May we reorient our lives around Christ, who makes all things new.[252]

Including you.

I will sing of your love and justice, LORD.
I will praise you with songs.

I will be careful to live a blameless life—
when will you come to help me?

I will lead a life of integrity in my own home.

I will refuse to look at anything vile and vulgar. I hate
all who deal crookedly; I will have nothing to do with them.

I will reject perverse ideas and stay away from every evil.

I will not tolerate people who slander their neighbors.
I will not endure conceit and pride.

I will search for faithful people to be my companions.
Only those who are above reproach will be allowed
to serve me.

I will not allow deceivers to serve in my house,
and liars will not stay in my presence.

Psalm 101:1–7

WE MUST BE FAITHFUL
FOR A LONG TIME

✟ **W**e live in a fast-food culture, a microwave media–driven milieu that prioritizes speed over substance.

The Church has not been immune to this go-fast-or-go-away proclivity. We want instant transformation, full Jesus-Christ-ness by dinner or your money back. But God honors those who, as Eugene Peterson says, demonstrate "a long obedience in the same direction."[253]

The author of Hebrews tells us to offer up a sacrifice of praise to God,[254] which includes not only good deeds but good speech, not only righteous living but righteous talking and righteous thinking. The author explains that the reason we're meant to live differently from the world is that "we do not have an enduring city, but we are looking for the city that is to come." [255] NIV

In his book, *Encounter God in the City*, pastor Randy White recalls the legacy of Christians in the early history after Christ:

Christians in first-century Rome routinely retrieved bodies from pits called *carnarii*, where Romans threw their dead captives as well as the carcasses of animals. These Christians gave them decent burials, leading to the transformation of social mores. In the second century, female leaders of the church in Cairo retrieved abandoned infants from alleys and back roads and brought them to the public square where they sat under pagan statues and acted as wet nurses to them, saving their lives while sending a clear message to the populace of the city of the contrast between Christianity and pagan culture.[256]

We are compelled by Christ to work toward gathering lost souls and rescuing children, binding up the brokenhearted and mending the weak, bringing together the strays and the weirdos and the rejects, never turning away one of God's lost dogs.

That's why we're here. That's what we're for. To redeem. To restore. To cooperate. To create. To dream. And to make it all better.

With God's help.

For God's glory.

Create in me a clean heart, O God. Renew a loyal spirit within me. Do not banish me from your presence, and don't take your Holy Spirit from me.

Restore to me the joy of your salvation, and make me willing to obey you. Then I will teach your ways to rebels, and they will return to you. Forgive me for shedding blood, O God who saves; then I will joyfully sing of your forgiveness. Unseal my lips, O Lord, that my mouth may praise you.

You do not desire a sacrifice, or I would offer one. You do not want a burnt offering. The sacrifice you desire is a broken spirit. You will not reject a broken and repentant heart, O God.

Psalm 51:10–17

TIME TO
ROLL UP
YOUR SLEEVES

That's it. That's the longest and fullest explanation I can give for why it's up to you. God won't do for you what you won't endeavor for yourself. You gotta try, and God will help. You gotta do the work before God will bless it. It's your life. The dreams and the plans you have are yours alone. No one else will satisfy you. No one else will make you happy. They are not the answer. Neither are they the obstacle. They are the beneficiaries. But the fire in your belly belongs to you, belongs inside you, and is yours alone to tend.

So let it burn.

Stoke it. Let it get white hot.

You are a wild beast with a halo stapled to your soul. You were meant to dive headlong into the hurricane of your loves and your dreams. You were never meant to be domesticated. You were never meant to be safe or normal or well-behaved.

Seize your life. Set it on fire. Live with passion and intensity. Pursue your dreams. Climb mountains. Explore. Play outside. Write. Make love.

Because the future is yours, and you can make it what you wish. God gave us a Garden but requires from us a City. What kind of City are you making, sister? What kind of world do you envision, brother?

God is the Light that can't ever go out, but we don't have to wait for the end in order to drive off the darkness. Even a little light will do that. God has given us the Light of the Spirit. Ours is the lamp on the stand, illuminating the world. We are the Light in the Darkness. We are the flame in the night. We are the City on the hill.

And we will never diminish.

Because the world and the work is ours.

And if it's not the world you want, then you'd better get to work.

A SUMMARY OF NEW CREATION ESCHATOLOGY
AND SHALOMIC TELEOLOGY

The Bible begins in Eden, a Garden temple in which human beings served as priests and protectors. Our spiritual ancestors, Adam and Eve, were tasked with the ongoing development and maturation of the earth. Perhaps the simplest way to say this is to acknowledge that the Creator created creators to perpetuate Creation.

God made us to be like God.

We were designed to gather resources, release potential, and bring wise order to the world. We are meant to ensure that God's government, God's creativity, and God's peace cover the earth,

The world and the work is ours.

Everything we do, we do in cooperation with God, The Bible uses a metaphor to describe the specifically human portion of this work: the City. When we employ our imagination, our agency, and our relationships to further complexify and beautify Creation, we are working on the City in obedience to our divine mandate to fill the earth and subdue it.

Thus, God gave us a Garden but requires from us a City.

The archetypal City to which all humanity aspires is the New Jerusalem coming down from Heaven to cover the earth with the glory of God.

But this aspiration has been interrupted.

Sin short-circuited God's gameplan for divine-human cooperation. Adam and Eve, our spiritual ancestors, were expelled from Eden. God cursed their son Cain. Cain fled from God and founded the first City, counterfeiting God's gameplan. Other cities followed suit. Yet God did not abandon the project of human development. God did not forget our cities but entered them.

God has placed us within our cities to work for the good of the world. Cities are the engines and multipliers of human flourishing. Cities are amplifiers of human culture. A right spirit can heal our cities, and our work in cities now anticipates God's final redemptive work in all cities later on.

Every City has icons and idols—things that point to God and things that point away from God. When we chase our idols, we become commodified, and this creates dis-ease.

The church is the City of God amid the cities of men. We are not technically a place but a culturally distinct people. We live as the City in the City and are called to show the world a better way to live.

Together.

We are citizens of Heaven but live on earth as resident aliens. Our true citizenship is revealed in the way we live; and, in all things, we demonstrate that Christ is our Lord through our obedience to his Way.

God's gameplan requires we remain faithful for a long time before we will see lasting results. Like Abraham, we yearn for the City whose architect and builder is God, the City ultimately given in full and final fulfillment of the Edenic mandate, so God's glory covers the earth.

NOTES

[1] Genesis 1:26–27.

[2] 2 Corinthians 5:20.

[3] The Hebrew word *tselem*, often translated "image" ("let us make man in our image"), can also be rendered as "shadows." See James Strong, *Strong's Expanded Exhaustive Concordance of the Bible* (Nashville: Thomas Nelson, 2009), s.v. "image" (H6754).

[4] Athanasius, *On the Incarnation*, Section 54: 93, accessed June 27, 2014, http://www.ccel.org/ccel/athanasius/incarnation. (paraphrased)

[5] Genesis 1:28.

[6] Habakkuk 2:14.

[7] Genesis 1:28.

[8] Genesis 2:20.

[9] Genesis 4:22.

[10] Exodus 31:1–11.

[11] The New Jerusalem, also called "the holy city," is not a place but a people. That's why John the Revelator refers to the New Jerusalem as the Bride of Christ in Revelation 21:9, 10. The Apostle Peter's reference to Christians as "'living stones'" in 1 Peter 2:5 gets to much the same point. John develops this image, describing those who join Jesus in heaven ruling as kings over the earth, employing language that elicits dominion (cf. Revelation 5:9–10; 21:2). The work we do in the holy city, as the holy city, is foreshadowed here and now on earth. This is as it should be, given that God's instruction to us in the Creation mandate of Genesis 2 requires we "fill the earth and govern it." Likewise, there were many prophetic admonitions to build and work and live developmentally. For example, Jeremiah 29.5–7, instructs the people of God to build homes and live in them, etc. When we do that, we're doing "City-work." In our present state, all such City-work is partial, incomplete, corrupted, etc. But, eschatologically, our City-work will be redeemed, restored, sanctified. But the part of this work that we can control—the part that we have been commanded to undertake—is the same both now and in eternity since in Revelation we

ARE the City, we LIVE in the City, and the WORK we do is City-work.

[12] Revelation 21.

[13] "The Garden," in this book, is the world—every fig and fjord and all the fecundity therein. Synonyms for the Garden include: Earth, the world, and Creation. "Eden" is the literal parcel of land God first entrusted to Adam and Eve. We might, figuratively, refer to Eden meaning "the longing human beings have for their original habitat," but the great majority of uses simply means the beginning location for human beings.

[14] "The City" is shorthand for our work in the world, which includes drawing together the resources of Creation, bringing wise order to the Garden, and releasing human potential.

[15] Revelation 21:2.

[16] 1 Peter 2:5.

[17] Ephesians 3:17.

[18] 1 Corinthians 3:16.

[19] 1 Corinthians 3:11.

[20] Ephesians 2:20.

[21] Since much of this thinking originates in the Old Testament Genesis, I am referring to "'God'" rather than specifying "'Jesus.'" However, most of my theological underpinnings are Christologically rooted in the New Testament. Please forgive my free exchange of trinitarian nomenclature and trust that I'll continue to clarify as we progress through the book.

[22] Stephen T. Um and Justin Buzzard, *Why Cities Matter: To God, the Culture, and the Church* (Wheaton, IL: Crossway, 2013), 58.

[23] **Paradise (n.)** late Old English, "the garden of Eden," from Old French *paradis* "paradise, garden of Eden" (11c.), from Late Latin *paradisus* "a park, an orchard; the garden of Eden, the abode of the blessed," from Greek *paradeisos* "a park; paradise, the garden of Eden," from an Iranian source similar to Avestan *pairidueza* "enclosure, park" (Modern Persian and Arabic *firdaus* "garden, paradise"), a compound of *pairi-* "around" (from PIE root ***per-** (1) "forward," hence "in front of, near, against, around") + *diz* "to make, to form (a wall)." The first element is cognate with Greek *peri* "around, about" (see **per**), the second is from PIE root ***dheigh-** "to form, build." See https://www.etymonline.com/search?q=paradise. See also Alexis C. Madrigal, "Good News, Facebook! The Root Word

for 'Paradise' Originally Meant 'Walled Garden,'" *The Atlantic*, July 20, 2012, https://www.theatlantic.com/technology/archive/2012/07/good-news-facebook-the-root-word-for-paradise-originally-meant-walled-garden/260140/.

[24] Joshua J. Mark, "Enuma Elish—The Babylonian Epic of Creation," World History Encyclopedia, May 4, 2018, http://www.ancient.eu/article/225/.

[25] G. K. Beale, *The Temple and the Church's Mission: A Biblical Theology of the Dwelling Place of God* (Downers Grove, IL: InterVarsity Press, 2004), 26.

[26] James Strong, *Strong's Expanded Exhaustive Concordance of the Bible* (Nashville: Thomas Nelson, 2009), s.v. "image" (H6754).

[27] Beale, *Temple and the Church's Mission*, 68.

[28] Ibid., 85.

[29] This will become significant later on, when the serpent enters the temple and brings uncleanness with him.

[30] 1 Peter 2:9.

[31] "Original Blessing" was first coined by Matthew Fox in his book by the same name. Matthew Fox, *Original Blessing: A Primer in Creation Spirituality Presented in Four Paths, Twenty-Six Themes, and Two Questions* (New York: TarcherPerigee, 2009).

[32] Genesis 1:28.

[33] Genesis 2:19.

[34] Harvie M. Conn and Manuel Ortiz, *Urban Ministry: The Kingdom, the City & the People of God* (Downers Grove, IL: InterVarsity Press, 2001), 87.

[35] Psalm 91.

[36] Psalm 32:8; 119:105.

[37] Robert D. Lupton, *Toxic Charity: How Churches and Charities Hurt Those They Help (And How to Reverse It)* (New York: HarperCollins, 2011), 154.

[38] Ibid., 152.

[39] James Strong, *Strong's Expanded Exhaustive Concordance of the Bible* (Nashville: Thomas Nelson, 2009), s.v. "avodah" (H5656).

[40] There is some reason to caution against workaholism if families are exploited, rest is ignored, and spirits are depleted. But this chapter is to remind us work can be wonderful.

[41] In fulfillment of Habakkuk 2:14.

[42] Tim Keller, "A Biblical Theology of the City," *Evangelicals Now* (July 2002): 5.

[43] Revelation 21:1.

[44] Um and Buzzard, *Why Cities Matter*, 58.

[45] Ibid.

[46] This is the thesis of Peter H. Diamandis and Steven Kotler's brilliant book *Abundance: Why the Future Is Better Than You Think*, and a key underpinning in Bill and Melinda Gates's 2014 annual letter for the Gates Foundation, "3 Myths that Block Progress for the Poor." Peter H. Diamandis and Steven Kotler, *Abundance: The Future Is Better Than You Think* (New York : Free Press, 2012). "3 Myths That Block Progress for the Poor," 2014 Gates Annual Letter, Bill and Melinda Gates Foundation, https://www.gatesfoundation.org/-/media/gfo/5ideas_articles/annual-letters/al2014-pdf-files/2014_gatesannualletter_english_1.pdf.

[47] See *cultivate*: by 1650s, of land, "till, prepare for crops;" by 1690s of crops, "raise or produce by tillage;" from Medieval Latin *cultivatus*, past participle of *cultivare* "to cultivate," from Late Latin *cultivus* "tilled," from Latin *cultus* "care, labor; cultivation," from past participle of *colere* "to cultivate, to till; to inhabit; to frequent, practice, respect; tend, guard," from PIE root ***kwel-** (1) "revolve, move round; sojourn, dwell." https://www.etymonline.com/search?q=cultivate.

   See also *culture* (n): mid-15c., "the tilling of land, act of preparing the earth for crops," from Latin *cultura* "a cultivating, agriculture," figuratively "care, culture, an honoring," from past participle stem of *colere* "to tend, guard; to till, cultivate" (see **colony**). Meaning "the cultivation or rearing of a crop, act of promoting growth in plants" (1620s) was transferred to fish, oysters, etc., by 1796, then to "production of bacteria or other microorganisms in a suitable environment" (1880), then "product of such a culture" (1884), https://www.etymonline.com/search?q=culture.

[48] Cf. 1 Kings 7:34; Isaiah 11:12; Ezekiel 7:2.

[49] Cf. Genesis 13:14; Deuteronomy 3:27; Ezekiel 7:2.

[50] Cf. Jeremiah 49:36; Ezekiel 37:9; Daniel 7:2.

[51] Cf. Ezekiel 1:5; Revelation 4:6.

[52] Cf. Exodus 20:8.

[53] Cf. Genesis 2:10–14: Pishon, Gihon, Tigris, and Euphrates.

54 Len Sweet, conversation with the author, March 2020. See also Leonard Sweet, *Me and We: God's New Social Gospel* (Nashville, TN: Abingdon Press, 2014).

55 Timothy Keller, *Center Church: Doing Balanced, Gospel-Centered Ministry in Your City* (Grand Rapids, MI: Zondervan, 2012), 150.

56 Ephesians 1:22.

57 Revelation 19:11-21. Note: the King's armies are never deployed and take no action.

58 John 3:16.

59 Philippians 2:7.

60 Revelation 4–5.

61 Mark 10:27.

62 Romans 8:37.

63 1 Peter 2:9.

64 1 Corinthians 12.

65 Psalm 46:1.

66 Revelation 21.

67 Revelation 21:2.

68 Genesis 1:26–31.

69 Revelation 21:3.

70 Psalm 22:3.

71 Colossians 3:23.

72 Joel 2:28; Ezekiel 36:27.

73 Revelation 21:16.

74 Psalm 24:1.

75 Revelation 22:2.

76 Revelation 21.

77 Revelation 21:5.

78 Genesis 2:16.

79 Exodus 16:1-3.

80 Matthew 26:14-16

81 Genesis 4:2–4.

82 Genesis 4:8.

83 Genesis 4:12.

84 Romans 5:1.

85 Ephesians 1:5.

86 Psalm 34:15.

87 Jacques Ellul, *The Meaning of the City*, trans. Dennis Pardee (Eugene, OR: Wipf & Stock, 1970), 4.

88 Genesis 4:21.

89 Genesis 4:22.

90 Genesis 4:17-22.

91 The city is 'iyr re'em. See Ellul, *Meaning of the City*, 9.

92 Ellul, *Meaning of the City*, 3.

93 Job 1:21. (paraphrased)

94 Conn and Ortiz, *Urban Ministry*, 86.

95 In an earlier chapter, we were introduced to the Hebrew word *tselem*, which can be translated as "image," "idol," "phantom," or "shadow." We identified that God's many prohibitions against idolatry were because of their insult not merely to God but also to humanity—for we are meant to be God's "idols." Here, let us acknowledge that *idols* is not an especially helpful term, given that very few of us are likely to appropriate it for ourselves, our churches, or our families. It's a word that's become oily, since so many have fingered it. Let us, instead, proclaim that we ought to be God's icons. An idol gathers worship for itself. An icon points glory to God.

96 Hebrews 11:10.

97 Conn and Ortiz, *Urban Ministry*, 84.

98 Habakkuk 3:2a. NIV

99 Jim Perkinson, "Theology and the City: Learning to Cry, Struggling to See," *CrossCurrents*, Spring 2001, https://www.academia.edu/647711/Theology_and_the_City_Learning_to_Cry_Struggling_to_See.

100 Genesis 3:8.

101 Genesis 1:28 30.

102 Revelation 21:22.

103 Revelation 21:23.

104 Colossians 3:10.

[105] C. 900 BCE, or possibly earlier.

[106] Numbers 35:6–8.

[107] Numbers 35:25; Deuteronomy 19:6. The avenger of blood was a blood relative of the deceased who was on a mission to claim an eye for an eye, a tooth for a tooth, and a life for a life (Deuteronomy 19:21). If the accused seeking asylum was found guilty by the elders in the city of refuge, they could still be handed over to the avenger of blood. Refuge didn't guarantee absolution, only justice in the form of a fair trial. They were not protected from prosecution, only from vengeance.

[108] Ellul, *Meaning of the City*, 101.

[109] John 6:33.

[110] John 3:17.

[111] John 12:47.

[112] Michael Mayne, *This Sunrise of Wonder* (London: Darton, Longman & Todd, 2008).

[113] Eugene Peterson, *The Message* (Colorado Springs, CO: NavPress, 2002).

[114] See https://www.oxfordreference.com/view/10.1093/acref/9780191826719.001.0001/q-oro-ed4-00010671.

[115] Rabbi Jonathan Sacks, *To Heal a Fractured World: The Ethics of Responsibility* (New York: Schocken Books, 2005), 72.

[116] Keller, *Center Church*, 140.

[117] 1 Corinthians 12:12–30.

[118] Crossan, John Dominic, *The Greatest Prayer: Rediscovering the Revolutionary Message of The Lord's Prayer*, (New York: HarperOne, 2010), 90.

[119] Sacks, *To Heal a Fractured World*, 77.

[120] Revelation 21:21.

[121] Luke records that Jesus "often withdrew to the wilderness for prayer" (5:16), but there are only six occasions in all the Gospels describing that he actually did so (six if you count the Mount of Transfiguration with Peter, James, and John). Clearly, Jesus was not prayer-less; though I find it fascinating how quickly modern readers assume Jesus was spending hours and hours every day alone. Granted, as a Jewish rabbi, he likely spent more time in prayer than the majority of modern Christians, but my point is that Jesus's prayer was

wedded to action, and we err when we separate the two as though our "prayer lives" and our "actions" are anything other than two chambers of the same heart.

122 1 Corinthians 9:24.

123 2 Timothy 2:5; Revelation 2:10.

124 Deuteronomy 30:19.

125 John 10:10.

126 Revelation 21:5.

127 Ephesians 2:4–6.

128 2 Timothy 2:12.

129 Revelation 5:13–14.

130 Revelation 20:4–6.

131 Revelation 2, 11.

132 Revelation 19:9, 17.

133 Revelation 2, 20.

134 Ecclesiastes 1:9.

135 Revelation 21:23.

136 Hebrews 13:8.

137 Wendell Berry, *The Art of the Commonplace: The Agrarian Essays of Wendell Berry*, ed. Norman Wirzba (Berkeley, CA: Counterpoint, 2002), 46.

138 Perkinson, "Theology and the City,".

139 Genesis 1:28.

140 Matthew 25:14–30.

141 1 Corinthians 10:31.

142 Seth Godin, "Work That Matters for People Who Care," Seth's Blog, October 18, 2018, https://seths.blog/2018/10/work-that-matters-for-people-who-care/.

143 Isaiah 6:3.

144 Ephesians 6:7.

145 Hebrews 11:10.

146 1 Corinthians 13:12.

147 George Eldon Ladd, *The Gospel of the Kingdom: Scriptural Studies in the Kingdom of God* (Grand Rapids, MI: Wm. B. Eerdmans, 1990).

148 Matthew 6:10.

149 Colossians 3:23.

150 1 Thessalonians 5:17.

151 1 Corinthians 12:27.

152 Luke 17:21.

153 Revelation 8:4.

154 Psalm 103:19.

155 Jeremiah 23:24.

156 Psalm 103:11.

157 John 17:3.

158 Revelation 21.

159 2 Peter 1:11.

160 Romans 8:17.

161 1 Peter 2:9.

162 John 10:10.

163 Revelation 11:15.

164 Revelation 21:2.

165 2 Timothy 2:12 promises those who "endure . . . will reign with [Christ]"; Revelation 5:10 promises the saints "will reign on the earth." According to Revelation 3:21, we will share Christ's throne, since Christ is uniting everything in himself through the fullness of his body, which is his church (see Ephesians 1:22–23).

166 In Revelation 21 John refers to the New Jerusalem as the Bride of Christ. But elsewhere, Christ's Bride is unambiguously defined as us—his people. We are the New Jerusalem. It's not a place, it's a people. Which means God makes his dwelling as much on us as in us. He lives in us like I live in Michigan.

167 Jon M. Dennis, *Christ + City: Why the Greatest Need of the City Is the Greatest News of All* (Wheaton, IL: Crossway, 2013), 147–49.

168 Daniel 4:22.

169 Luke 17:21.

170 Matthew 6:10.

171 Matthew 18:20.

172 Michael Wheeler, "Martin Heidegger," Stanford Encyclopedia of Philosophy, October 12, 2011, https://plato.stanford.edu/entries/heidegger/.

173 Belden C. Lane, *Landscapes of the Sacred: Geography and Narrative in American Spirituality*, expanded edition (Baltimore: Johns Hopkins University Press), v.

174 Isaiah 62:4.

175 Philippians 2:15.

176 1 John 2:15–17.

177 1 Timothy 2:1–15.

178 Matthew 18:1–4.

179 Luke 6:20.

180 Matthew 20:20–28.

181 Luke 6:27–28.

182 Matthew 6:25–34.

183 Luke 6:27–28.

184 Isaiah 51:11.

185 Revelation 11:15.

186 Matthew 3:2.

187 "Early Christian Writings: Epistle of Mathetes to Diognetus," accessed November 23, 2021, http://tutor1.net/wikiquote/122618.

188 Ibid., 6.1

189 Beale, *Temple and the Church's Mission*, 400.

190 2 Corinthians 2:15–17.

191 Second-century Church Father Tertullian, *Apologeticus*, accessed November 23, 2021, www.tertullian.org/works/apologeticum.htm.

192 Philippians 4:15–18.

193 Philippians 2:17.

194 Philippians 2:17.

195 1 Peter 2:10.

196 Keller, *Center Church*, 120.

197 Acts 13:13–43.

198 Acts 14:6–16.

[199] Acts 17:16–34.

[200] Acts 20:16–38.

[201] Acts 21:27–22:22.

[202] Acts 24–26.

[203] Colossians 1:18.

[204] Hebrews 12:1.

[205] Romans 12.5.

[206] Revelation 2:4.

[207] Ellul, *Meaning of the City*, 166–67.

[208] Revelation 5:10.

[209] Romans 4:17.

[210] Revelation 21:5.

[211] Revelation 6:2.

[212] Colossians 3:15.

[213] Matthew 11:5.

[214] Ephesians 4:5.

[215] John 15:5.

[216] For an accessible introduction to Zygmunt Bauman's work, see *Community: Seeking Safety in an Insecure World* (Cambridge, UK: Polity Press, 2001).

[217] Philippians 3:20.

[218] Romans 13:1: "Let everyone be subject to the governing authorities, for there is no authority except that which God has established. The authorities that exist have been established by God." NIV

[219] "Not only do God's people in the midst of the city already serve as God's presence, but much more important, they serve also as the temporal election of the city itself, to accomplish God's work. . . . By this means God gets a foothold in man's world" (Ellul, *Meaning of the City*, 90, 101).

[220] "Falsehood is the foundation of both the technician who thinks to make a city the ideal place for man's full development, equilibrium and virtue, and the politician who thinks to construct around giant cities the perfect society where men can get along without God" (Ibid., 130).

[221] Ephesians 1:10.

[222] 1 Corinthians 15:45.

[223] 2 Corinthians 5:17.

[224] "God intervenes in the world where man wanted to refuse him entrance" (Ellul, *Meaning of the City*, 101).

[225] 2 Corinthians 2:15.

[226] Acts 2:32.

[227] Matthew 5:14.

[228] 1 Peter 2:15.

[229] 1 Peter 2:11–15.

[230] Psalm 34:12–16.

[231] 1 Corinthians 15:28.

[232] David McDonald, *The Church Survival Guide: How to Be a Christian without Wishing You Could Start a New Religion* (self-pub., 2014), 113.

[233] Luke 16:13.

[234] 1 Timothy 5:8.

[235] Ecclesiastes 6:9–10.

[236] Ecclesiastes 5:18–20.

[237] 2 Corinthians 9:11.

[238] 2 Corinthians 9:7.

[239] Proverbs 19:17.

[240] Wayne A. Meeks, *The First Urban Christians: The Social World of the Apostle Paul*, (New Haven, CT: Yale University Press, 1983), 75.

[241] Joshua 24:15.

[242] Acts 16:25–40.

[243] Matthew 5:14.

[244] Isaiah 40:29–31.

[245] John 10:10.

[246] Revelation 7:10.

[247] Acts 2:21.

[248] Galatians 5:24.

[249] Romans 15:13.

[250] Isaiah 40:31.

[251] Matthew 8:16; Psalm 55:22; 1 Peter 5:10; 1 Corinthians 1:30; John 1:3.

[252] Revelation 21:5.

[253] Eugene Peterson, *A Long Obedience in the Same Direction: Discipleship in an Instant Society*, (Downers Grove, IL: InterVarsity Press, 2000).

[254] Hebrews 13:15–16.

[255] Hebrews 13:14.

[256] Randy White, *Encounter God in the City: Onramps to Personal and Community Transformation* (Downers Grove, IL: InterVarsity Press, 2006), 126–27.